More Praise for [illegible]

“*Come Back* is a captivating, motivating [illegible] inspiration to hope forward anew. Thro[illegible] real-life examples, and practical, user-fri[illegible] the pages seem to turn themselves. Give yourself the [illegible] of this engaging book, and gain a game plan for your own comeback!”

—Sue Nilson Kibbey, director of the Office of Missional Church Development, West Ohio Conference of The United Methodist Church

“Roger Ross has a heart for people. He has devoted his life and vocation to walking with people on the journey to being who they were intended to be. *Come Back* is fruit of his life’s work. Ross creatively intertwines the stories of real people with biblical narratives and time-tested literature. This is a ‘field guide’ to assist anyone to live an abundant life.”

—Gregory V. Palmer, resident bishop, Ohio West Episcopal Area of The United Methodist Church

“You CAN come back—from wherever it is you find yourself and from whatever set of circumstances have come your way. With one of Jesus’s most beloved stories serving as the backdrop, Roger Ross describes for us the anatomy of a comeback. If you’re looking for hope, you’ll love this book, because the next comeback can be your own!”

—Ron Watts, senior pastor, La Croix Church, Cape Girardeau, MO

“A very fine book full of engaging stories, terrific quotations, and biblical illustrations. What I hadn’t considered is how my own life could be viewed as a series of setbacks and comebacks—and how much I could benefit from just such a book. I know you will too.”

—Craig Hill, professor of New Testament and dean of Perkins School of Theology, Southern Methodist University, Dallas, TX

“The Christian journey is about comebacks. Addictions, divorce, bankruptcies, or moral failures need not define us. Our failures can become the arid desert journeys that lead us to God’s ultimate place of promise. In *Come Back: Returning to the Life You Were Made For,* Roger Ross inspires us through a descriptive, practical path for living the life we were made for.”

—Mike Slaughter, pastor emeritus of Ginghamsburg Church; founder and chief strategist of Passionate Churches, LLC

"*Come Back* makes me think. It makes me want to cheer. And it makes me want to change. Then it gives me tools to change that have been used successfully for thousands of years. Test it yourself. It may help you start your own turnaround story."

—Martha Grace Reese, author of the Unbinding the Gospel Series; Principal, MG Reese Associates, LLC

"Roger Ross is a church strategist and a 'thinking person's' evangelist. Compellingly and clearly, he points to real-time hope for anyone and everyone in need of a comeback. And let's face it, who doesn't need a comeback?"

—Shane L. Bishop, senior pastor, Christ Church, Fairview Heights, IL

"A carefully crafted masterpiece of amazing comeback stories. *Come Back* weaves together a series of remarkable snatched-from-the-jaws-of-defeat stories. Anchored by favorite biblical narratives, it's intertwined with makeover experiences most of us can easily relate to and identify with. Roger writes with a wealth of wisdom, passion, knowledge, and personal insight. He shares his own story of trust and surrender and gives helpful tips and tools geared to enable others to experience grace and ultimately inward transformation and personal comeback."

—Frank J. Beard, bishop, Illinois Great Rivers Conference of The United Methodist Church

"Like a motivating coach, Roger challenges us to rise after any setback in life. Every turn of the page comes with new insights from this timely book, all the while equipping us with the necessary spiritual tools to come back strong."

—Ken Nash, lead pastor, Watermark Wesleyan Church, Buffalo, NY

"Whether you are disinterested or delighting in God, *Come Back* is for you. You see, everyone in every place and in every time falters, fractures and fails at something in life. How does one rebound? Roger masterfully helps ordinary people with practical and timeless truth for honest and genuine recovery."

—Jorge Acevedo, lead pastor, Grace Church, southwest Florida

ROGER ROSS

Returning to the Life You Were Made For

Nashville

COME BACK:
RETURNING TO THE LIFE YOU WERE MADE FOR

Library of Congress Control Number: 2020935803
ISBN: 978-1-791-00818-5

20 21 22 23 24 25 26 27 28 29—10 9 8 7 6 5 4 3 2 1

MANUFACTURED IN THE UNITED STATES OF AMERICA

To my mom, Jeanette Ross

No matter the fall, around you
I always knew I could come back.

Contents

Acknowledgments

It caught me off guard. On a prayer retreat for other reasons, God whispered something. There was no audible voice. Just an impression. "Write about comebacks." I knew instantly the invitation was not because I was an expert, but because I needed one. After outlining some ideas, I shared them with Connie Stella at Abingdon. To my total surprise, she liked them. Before I knew it, I was writing a book.

With a short runway, any hope of getting this project off the ground depended on a COP—a Chief Outloud Processor. Thankfully, Patty Altstetter stepped up to the plate. She patiently listened as I bounced half-baked ideas off her left and right. Her wise counsel, prayer support, and occasional "Are you kidding me?" were a lifeline.

About halfway through, my friend, Richard Heyduck, read a draft and suggested a resource that completely changed the way I understood the prodigal son in Jesus's famous comeback story. His contribution was invaluable. When it came to the final editing, my new son-in-law, Sam Nichols, used his sports-writing and fact-checking prowess to offer excellent improvements. (It's great to have another writer in the family!) To at last take it to print, I'm thankful for the diligent editing and shepherding work of Katie Johnston and the Abingdon team.

A project like this is only possible because I work with fantastic people in the Missouri Conference of The United Methodist Church. I am deeply grateful for their support and for the leadership and encouragement of Bishop Bob Farr.

Finally, special thanks to my wife, Leanne, and our adult children, Zach and Jane. It takes true love to read multiple drafts of the same material while constantly being peppered with "How does this sound?" Your secret sacrifices prove your love.

Roger Ross

Introduction

It's Not Too Late

It's never too late—in fiction or in life—to revise.

—Nancy Thayer, American novelist

It wasn't supposed to happen. Sports writers that year called the Golden State Warriors a historic team—and for good reason. They won the NBA championship in 2015 only to come back the next year and set the record for regular season wins with a 73–9 mark.

Their star player, Steph Curry, had just won the MVP award for the second year running and had smashed the record for three-point buckets in a season.

As predicted, the Warriors cruised through the 2016 playoffs and found themselves in the finals with the Cleveland Cavaliers—again, the very team they beat the year before four games to two in a best-of-seven series.

A huge underdog, Cleveland's chances all but slipped away before they knew it. The Warriors jumped out to a 3–1 lead in the series. No team had ever rallied from a 3–1 deficit to win the NBA finals. Not one. To make matters worse, they were lugging around the weight of hometown history. Cleveland had not won a major sports championship since 1964.

To everyone's surprise, the Cavaliers won games 5 and 6 convincingly. Their star player, LeBron James, dropped 41 points each night to lead the way. With the series tied at 3–3, they headed back to the Warriors's home court for a deciding game 7.

Fans stood from the opening minutes. It was a seesaw battle with the Warriors taking a seven-point lead into halftime. The Cavs came back in the third quarter to regain the lead, then lose it again. Tied at 89 with a minute to play, Kyrie Irving drained a three-pointer that put Cleveland ahead. LeBron added a free throw. As the final seconds ticked off, the Cavaliers won 93–89!

The whole Cavalier team stormed the court. Cleveland fans lost their minds with joy. It was the Cavaliers's first championship in franchise history.

It may also have been the most triumphant return of a prodigal son any city has ever seen. Drafted by Cleveland in 2003, LeBron James left the Cavaliers in 2010 to play for the Miami Heat. The news crushed Cleveland fans. As a native of Akron, Ohio, James was one of theirs. He was "the One" who was supposed to bring the glory back. He instantly became a traitor. After cheering him for years, they now burned his jersey in effigy.

While in Miami, James won two NBA championships. But in 2014, James decided on a second coming to Cleveland. In a postgame interview after the improbable win, he explained why: "I came back for a reason. I came back to bring a championship to our city."[1] Now it all made sense. When asked why this championship felt different, James offered a two-word reply: "I'm home."[2]

I have a confession to make. I love comebacks. I always have. I love it when a sports team or a business, a church or a neighborhood turns it all around. Perhaps they've had some bad breaks. Maybe the team or the area has been in decline for some time, and people have lost hope.

"Well, back in the day, they were really something, but that was a long time ago."

Just when everyone had counted them out, the team wins a game, the company shows a profitable quarter, someone has a life-changing encounter with God, a family moves in and renovates their house. Before you know it, the same thing happens again, and again. Momentum shifts, and a comeback is born.

Comebacks touch us on a soul level. There's something within us that instinctively roots for the underdog. It connects with the part inside us that's always playing against the odds. We want them to win, so we can win too. Deep down, we know we were made for a turnaround.

We marvel when someone like LeBron James brings an NBA title to Cleveland after a fifty-two-year sports drought or Apple Inc. goes from near bankruptcy in 1997 to one of the most valuable companies in the world, but most of us are facing challenges that will never hit headline news. They are private, deep, and very real. My new friend Shane Laswell gives a chilling example from his life.

> About six months or so before my fourteenth birthday, I'm lying on the bed in our spare bedroom. I'm on my stomach playing Nintendo. My dad comes in, jumps on our bed, and starts choking me. I could feel his hands getting tighter and tighter. I have never been so scared in my life. I knew I was done. I knew I was going to die.
>
> Next thing I know, here comes my mom, home from work early. She ends up pushing him off. And that night when we

were pulling out of the driveway, I remember being in that truck. We had just set the back tires down in the street, and she said, "Hey, I've got to tell you something I should have told you a long time ago. Mark isn't your dad."

I just wanted to numb everything. I didn't want any of these things that had happened to my life to ever affect me, and I knew the one way not to have them affect me was to use—and to use more.

At that time, I drank almost every day. At least every other day. But then I started seeking out harder drugs and got introduced to meth. I kept meth and pills from the age of eighteen until twenty days before my thirty-ninth birthday. I didn't care if I lived or died from day to day, but I knew I had a plan I would execute right after March.

I drained my bank account of all the cash I had and went to a hotel on April 5, 2012. I knew that this was it. I was done. My letter was already written to my family. I loaded up the syringe and went into the bathroom to shoot up with the sole purpose of not caring if I woke up. Hoping I wouldn't wake up.

The next day I woke up still alive.

Push pause right there. If you were Shane, what would you do next? Try to numb the pain again? Cry out, "Why?" Ask, "What am I supposed to do with my life now?" I know he sorted through those options and more. But ultimately, he made some courageous choices he will describe in a later chapter—choices that led to a completely new life.

Are there places in your life where you need a comeback? Not just the kind where you score a bunch of points at the end of a game. Perhaps so many things have happened to you, your journey has taken you to such a distant place, that you are no longer yourself. Maybe what you need most is to *come back*, to return home to the life you were made for. Perhaps your journey has been around family brokenness or a friend's betrayal. It could be classmate drama or a painful divorce. Maybe money problems or health issues have thrown you for a loss. Whatever the case, life has been running up the score against you, and it feels like you can't come back. How do you turn it around?

As we walk through these pages together, I'll share five elements crucial to every comeback. Each element is paired with an ancient practice that has helped people for thousands of years in countless cultures navigate the tricky waters of transformation. Although this process can be traced back a long way, every new turnaround follows a version of this path. Here's a quick rundown of the journey.

1. **You Fall** I know. I don't like this part either. Things are going along nicely, and suddenly, you fall—badly. It may be a disaster that hits you out of the blue, but more often it's a decision you make or something you do, something you now regret. In each case, you face a choice. Will you allow that fall to define and defeat you, or will you choose to dig deeper, ignite hope, and mount a comeback?
    - **Transforming Practice: Listen to Your Emotions** Most of us are woefully unaware of what we really feel about our lives and experiences. If we do have some inkling, we tend to numb our emotions to escape the pain, or we ignore them for fear they might slow us down. Those unidentified or buried emotions often drive us into a free fall or keep us mired in a fall's aftermath

years after the fact. Learning how to listen to our emotions without letting them control us is a key that unlocks the door to a new life.

2. **You Come to Yourself** After a seemingly endless free fall, you finally hit bottom and experience an "Aha!" moment. You suddenly see your life for what it has become and know something *has* to change. When you come to yourself, you make a deep internal decision: "I'm not staying here anymore. I refuse to wallow in this emotional slop for the rest of my life. I was made for more than this." Grasping this truth sets you on a new course.
   - **Transforming Practice: Choose Solitude and Stillness** Each year the pace of life gets faster. More is expected in less time at higher quality. Frenzied busyness leaves no margin for rest, reflection, or connection. We meet ourselves coming and going yet feel more and more distant from the person in the mirror we once knew. Practicing times of solitude and stillness gives us the space to see ourselves for who we really are—and to decide to do something about it.

3. **You Find a Guide** The road back is long and winding, with lots of peaks and pitfalls. The best way to navigate it is with a guide. You will need someone, perhaps several someones, who can offer wise counsel. Like a long hike through an uncharted stretch of dense jungle, this trek is too difficult to make by yourself. Find a guide who can point the way.
   - **Transforming Practice: Seek Wise Counsel** At some deep level, this conversation takes place in nearly every human being, "No one knows my situation better than I do. Why talk to someone

else about it? I just need to figure it out." Although this sounds right, it does not take into consideration the crucial issues we can't see about ourselves that are undermining our lives. We have blind spots. Seeking wise counsel from trusted people helps us overcome them.

4. **You Make a Plan and Take Action** It's not enough to have a clear destination. You need a plan to get from here to there. The very act of making a plan will increase your comeback chances exponentially, even if you need to adapt it along the way. Your guide(s) can help you here. Keep in mind, people fall much faster than they rise. Making your way back will not happen all at once. The pace may feel glacial at times. Even so, you must take action as soon as possible. Action creates momentum. Momentum makes your next step ten times easier.

   - **Transforming Practice: Plan and Act** There are two kinds of people. Those who like to plan and those who like to act. But a plan without action is just as ineffective as action without a plan. The key to moving the comeback needle is a healthy balance of both.

5. **You Trust the Process** If you choose to make a comeback bid, prepare yourself to wander in a wilderness for a while. Both inwardly and outwardly, you will struggle with great doubt over whether you *can* come back. Many people get partway there and give up. Don't be one of them. Doubt is the leading edge of faith. Faith is the unseen secret of turnarounds. Simply own this fact: no struggle, no comeback. Real struggle winnows out your false hopes and makes room for deep faith to carry you through the messy middle to a new life.

- **Transforming Practice: Embrace Patient Trust**
  I have yet to meet a person who likes to stand in line. When it comes to the practice of patience, it's great as long as we can see the results right now! Embracing patient trust involves a willingness to let things develop on their own timeline instead of ours.

These five practices of the comeback journey are designed for everyday people to make a turnaround from where they are to where they want to be. Anyone can do any one of them. However, true transformation comes when the practices are done collectively.

You may be thinking, "But you don't know my situation. You don't know how bad it is or how long it's been this way. I think I missed my window." True. I don't. But chances are you picked up this book because you—or someone you love—long to return to the life you were made for. If so, there is good news. It's not too late, and you're not too far. The mere fact that you are reading these words shows you are more ready than you think. What you have always suspected deep down is true. You were made for a comeback.

Before we go any further, full disclosure—I am a pastor. I've been a follower of Jesus for many years. To be honest, I shudder to think what my life would look like apart from the transforming love of Christ. But what's before you is not intended to be a "Christian" book for a simple reason: Christians are not the only ones who need a comeback at some point.

These words are not only for people of faith but also for people who have never gone to church, people who used to go, and people who carry scars from church gone wrong. It's for those who strongly believe in God and those who strongly don't. Although I will draw from biblical wisdom, there is no prerequisite of religious convictions. Like the prodigal son in one of Jesus's most famous stories, you don't need a spiritual pedigree to start the journey. Here's what you do need: a heartfelt desire to see your life turn around and an openness to the process. That's it. The rest will be revealed along the way.

Chapter 1
It Was Going So Well

The longest journey
is the journey inwards.

—Dag Hammarskjöld

He transcended the game. You didn't have to play golf, like it, or even watch it on TV to recognize his patented fist pump or final-round red shirt. Bursting on the scene like fireworks in midsummer, he ignited polite crowds with his power, precision, and passion on the links.

In 1996, the PGA named him Rookie of the Year. In 1997, he won his first Masters Tournament at age twenty-one—by twelve strokes. He went on to dominate the world of golf in jaw-dropping fashion. During one stretch in 2000–2001, he won four major championships in a row. Only Bobby Jones had won four straight—back in 1930.

By 2008, he had collected fourteen majors, a feat surpassed only by Jack Nicklaus's mark of eighteen. At age thirty-two, he was poised to smash Jack's record and claim the title to which he had dedicated his life: Greatest Golfer of All Time.

As tournament wins stacked up, endorsement contracts poured in like birdie putts. He was the first athlete in history to earn $1 billion. Beyond extreme wealth, he was on track to become the most well-known athlete in the world—bigger than Muhammad Ali or Michael Jordan.

At the end of 2009, the Associated Press named him Athlete of the Decade, a fit coronation for his play. In September of that year he won the season-culminating FedEx Cup for the second time and was named PGA Player of the Year for the tenth time.

He also appeared happily married to Swedish model Elin Nordegren and absolutely adored their two young children, Sam and Charlie.

To say Tiger Woods's life was going well would have been the understatement of the century.

Then came November 27, 2009. Reports surfaced about a car accident in the early morning hours near Tiger's Florida home. His Escalade ran into a fire hydrant. He incurred facial lacerations along with a traffic citation but refused to see the police. Soon after, Tiger announced on his website he would bow out of the upcoming tournament he was hosting. Something was wrong. Five days later, a cocktail waitress claimed a two-and-a-half-year affair with Woods. Within a couple of weeks, fourteen more women came forward, including a porn star. It was just the beginning.

For his part, Woods publicly admitted "transgressions" and expressed sorrow over how he had let down his family and hurt his wife. It was too little too late.

As salacious details of infidelity hit headlines everywhere, Tiger's carefully cultivated reputation evaporated. Longtime sponsors including Accenture, Gillette, AT&T, and Gatorade dropped him like a rock. Studies showed that shareholders associated with

Woods lost over $10 billion. The following year, Tiger and his wife, Elin, divorced.

It was the greatest fall from grace in modern sports history. Its speed and severity were at once breathtaking and heartbreaking. The most brilliant fourteen-year run in sports came crashing down in a matter of weeks.

Undoubtedly, few people on the planet can relate to a fall of this magnitude, but all of us know what it is like for things to be going well until one day they don't.

In *The Sun Also Rises*, Ernest Hemingway describes this uniquely human experience:

> "How did you go bankrupt?" Bill asked.
> "Two ways," Mike said. "Gradually and then suddenly."

In four words, Hemingway explains the nature of self-inflicted falls. While some tumbles are beyond our control—wars, pandemics, economic downturns—self-inflicted falls follow this pattern precisely: gradually, then suddenly.

It's the subtleness that catches us—like the frog in a kettle. Place a frog in a pot of hot water, and he will immediately jump out. Replace it with room temperature water, and he will sit there with a smile. But if you slowly turn up the heat, one degree at a time, he'll sit there until he's boiled. Gradual adjustments are often imperceptible until it's too late.

"I have to work late again tonight. She'll understand."

"A few puffs on a cigarette won't kill me."

"Another credit card would really help me spread my spending around."

It's gradual. On any given day, choices like these would barely move the needle. But slowly, over months and years, they create an invisible force that eats away at the foundation of our lives like termites. When a "sudden" fall hits, we almost never see it coming.

Jesus tells a story like this. A younger son gets bored down on the farm. Desperate to find a life, he makes a shocking request. "Father, give me my part of the estate." Jesus's original listeners would have gasped at these words. In effect, he was saying, "Old man, I wish you were dead, but you're not. I can't wait any longer, so give me my share of your money now."

Stunningly, the father complies. The younger son promptly sets off on the road trip of his life to find himself. With cash falling from his pockets, friends flock to him. For a time, he lights up the town in what one Bible version calls "riotous living."[1] (Fill in your own blanks.) Before long, the money runs out, and so do his friends.

Just then a major economic downturn hits. Broke, starving, and far from home, he convinces a local farmer to hire him. As a final indignity, he finds himself feeding pigs, the most disgusting job a Jewish person could imagine.[2] Every day he goes to work thinking, "No one back home knows where I am or what I am doing. They probably don't even care." Each day he feels a little further from himself than the day before. He doesn't know where to turn. The younger son could never have imagined falling this far this fast.

Can you relate? People say experience is the best teacher. That's only half true. Evaluated experience is the best teacher. Taking the time to reflect on what happened, dig into what caused it, and feel the full range of emotions around the fall are how we leverage an experience and create a new future.

Let's break that down. Most of us are blindly unaware of the feelings that drive us into poor decisions or destructive behaviors. All we know is we want to feel good, so we pursue those things we think will help us achieve that goal. For Americans, this shouldn't be a surprise. It's written into our national DNA—life, liberty, and the pursuit of happiness.

Naturally, when we fall, we feel bad. Sometimes we feel so bad, we don't know if we will ever get back up. In nearly all cases, our feelings will either sabotage a comeback or be the stepping stones to a new future.

One of my favorite windows into the power of our emotions is Pixar's incredibly creative movie *Inside Out*.

The heroine of the story is eleven-year-old Riley. Her birth sparks the first emotion, Joy. As she grows, other emotions emerge to help her navigate life: Sadness, Fear, Anger, and Disgust. They all have a crucial role to play, but it is Joy who takes charge of the team to ensure Riley's happiness at every point.[3]

The emotions live in a control room in Riley's mind and are responsible for making sure her core memories are protected. As the movie opens, everything is going along quite well in Riley's life. She lives with her mom and dad in a quiet country home in Minnesota where happy memories multiply like rabbits in the spring.

But everything changes when the family moves from Minnesota to a townhouse in San Francisco. Riley is distraught over the loss of her friends and former life, and she begins to rebel against her parents. This throws her emotions into a tailspin.

Joy is consumed with preserving the happiness of Riley's core memories and does everything she can to keep Sadness from tainting them with her touch. But in a scuffle, Riley's core memories (contained in large, shining balls) fall all over the control room and are accidentally sucked up a tube that goes to long-term memory. Joy and Sadness get vacuumed up the tube with them. This leaves Anger, Fear, and Disgust in control of Riley's life. You can imagine where this is going.

We all know how difficult it is when our emotions are all over the map. One day I met with a family who had lost their beloved father and grandfather. As we planned the memorial service, a stream of precious memories poured out. There were so many happy times, so many amazing stories of his life, we all felt the sadness of losing this dear man.

Two minutes later, another family came in with their bouncing baby boy to talk about baptism. The parents let me hold this seven-month-old, twenty-three-pound bruiser on my lap as he smiled a toothless grin and played with his feet. (He had just discovered them the week before.)

Talk about an emotional head jerk. In the span of minutes, I went from real sadness to pure joy. Maybe you've had days when your emotions took you on a wild ride.

Let's assume for a moment that Pixar is on to something and that there are various emotions vying for a front row seat in the control center of your brain. Each one would take you down a very different path if it got the chance. How do you manage these crazy characters?

There are four basic ways people deal with their emotions.

Run with Them

Some people just run with their emotions. Whatever they feel, they do. Some might say they wear their heart on their sleeve.

They laugh, they cry, they get mad—all in the blink of an eye. You never have to wonder what they are feeling. There are lots of good things about that. These people tend to be more natural and authentic. They can be easy to trust because they are not trying to hide anything.

The downside of turning our lives over to our emotions is a lack of impulse control. We see something we want, we buy it. We get bored with a relationship, we jump into another one. Someone says something we don't like, we blow up at that person on the spot. We feel sad about something, we barricade ourselves in our room for three days.

Our lives are spent reacting. It's like living on Disney's Space Mountain roller-coaster ride. We have no control over whether we are going up or down, left or right; and it's too dark to see what's coming next. We're just holding on for dear life, hoping we will get to the end in one piece.

When we run with our emotions, our emotions end up running us.

The opposite end of the spectrum is to hide them.

Hide Them

Some people see emotions as dangerous. *E–motions* have a way of "energizing motion," so you never know what they might lead you to do. Rather than embrace their emotions, these people shun them. They try to lock them in a closet in their heart, hoping to hide them from view. This often happens in Christian groups because people are afraid of what others might think or how it would look if "unacceptable" emotions were expressed.

John describes a poignant turnaround in his own spiritual journey:

> Although I had been a Christian over ten years, I hid from my wretchedness, my defenses, my broken parts, even the abuse I suffered as a young boy. In fact, I was always hiding—hiding my anger, jealousy, arrogance, conditional love, selfishness, brokenness, mistakes, weaknesses, and inadequacies. These things were unacceptable in the Christian circles I knew, especially among leaders. I didn't think I would be liked or accepted if I was not strong and together. Who would then listen to me? I had to prove myself capable, strong, perfect, and confident.
>
> . . . I unconsciously had what people call the daisy mentality—"He loves me, He loves me not. He loves me, he loves me not"—based on how well I was doing in my spiritual life.
>
> Through a study of Galatians (in the Bible), I received a fresh and powerful grasp of the gospel of Jesus Christ. I don't have to prove myself to anyone—which is how I was unconsciously living my life. I am perfectly loved and accepted by God because of Christ's life, death, and resurrection for me. . . . I can actually be free to be me. I can come out of hiding!
>
> I am free to fail, to share my weaknesses and needs with others, to admit if I have a problem, to say "I don't know," to admit "I was wrong, please forgive me," to recognize that I don't have all the answers, and to relax and have fun, not thinking I have to take care of everyone else.[4]

Ever known someone who had a daisy mentality with God? The truth Jesus came to share is that you and I don't have to prove ourselves to anyone—not even to God. I like the way Max Lucado says it:

> If I'm better tomorrow, I won't be loved more.
> If I'm worse tomorrow, I won't be loved less.
> God's love does not ebb and flow or come and go.[5]

That's grace—God's unmerited favor. It means there is nothing you can do to make God love you more—or less—than God does right now. We are treasured and loved in God's eyes. We need only to accept that love. That's how we come out of hiding.

However, you may not run with your emotions or hide them. You may prefer to run from them.

Run from Them

Do you know people who are always busy, always overcommitting, always overworking? When they come to the end of one activity, they dive into two more. Or perhaps you know people who are constantly distracting themselves. They're in sports leagues four or five nights a week, always in the next play or musical, consumed with a hobby, or out with their friends every night. Maybe they spend a ton of time at church or their favorite pub. When they're in the car, their playlist is always cranked. When they work out, their headphones are always on. When they come home, the first thing switched on is their TV. And no matter where they are, their nose is in their phone.

Outwardly, there's never a time when they are alone and still. What's driving that? It could be they are trying to escape their emotions.

A wise professor of mine used to say, "The busiest people in life are the deadest."

I thought, "That can't be true. Busy people are the ones who get things done. They bring things to life!"

Only later did I realize what he meant. They may be creating a whirlwind of activity on the outside, but they are dead on the inside. They stagger through life like zombies, no longer alive but relentlessly on the move. They don't take time to slow down, to feel, and to listen. That's what makes this final approach to our emotions so powerful.

Listen to Them

In *The Cry of the Soul*, Dan Allender and Tremper Longman explain the power behind listening to and dealing with our emotions:

> Ignoring our emotions is turning our back on reality; listening to our emotions ushers us into reality. And reality is where we meet God. . . . Emotions are the language of the soul. They are the cry that gives the heart a voice. . . . However, we often turn a deaf ear—through emotional denial, distortion, or disengagement. We strain out anything disturbing in order to gain tenuous control of our inner world. We are frightened and ashamed of what leaks into our inner world. *In neglecting our intense emotions, we are false to ourselves and lose a wonderful opportunity to know God.* We forget that change comes through brutal honesty and vulnerability before God.[6]

We don't often talk about this, but emotions play a crucial role in a person's spiritual journey. It's through our emotions that we feel the presence of God, sense the sorrow over our own wrongs, experience the inexpressible joy of forgiveness, and feel our heart break with compassion for those who are far from God spiritually, those who are suffering physically, and those who are hurting relationally.

Without emotions, our faith would be as dry as toast. Watch where this story leads.

A little girl was sitting on her grandfather's lap as he read her a bedtime story. From time to time, she would take her eyes off the book and reach up to touch his wrinkled cheek. Back and forth she would stroke her own cheek, then his again.

Finally, she spoke up, "Grandpa, did God make you?"

"Yes, sweetheart," he said, "God made me a long time ago."

"Oh," she paused, "Grandpa, did God make me too?"

"Yes, indeed, honey," he said, "God made you just a little while ago."

Feeling each of their faces again, she said, "I think God's getting better at it."

What are you feeling right now? Joy. How does that compare with dead seriousness all the time? Would you like to make that trade?

Did you know there used to be laws in some states saying ministers could not tell jokes in church? That's what the eighteenth-century Enlightenment thinkers did to Christianity. They sucked the emotions right out of faith.

They believed what makes a person human is one's rational ability, and they belittled emotions. Their mantra was: "I think, therefore I am." As a result, for over two centuries in the West, Christianity was something you did from the neck up. It was all about right doctrine, getting people to think the right way about God. Emotions were suspect, somehow subhuman.

But that's changing now. Author and professor George Hunter says:

> With the fading of the Enlightenment and the rise of post-modern thought, it is becoming apparent that the Enlightenment was wrong by almost 180 degrees. We are not basically rational creatures who sometimes feel; we are basically emotional creatures who sometimes

> think. Even what we think about is influenced by our background emotional state, and how we think about it is influenced by our feelings at the time.[7]

To anyone connected to the Methodist faith, this isn't new. John Wesley, Methodism's founder, talked almost daily about what he called "religious affections," our feelings about God. He defined Christianity as essentially "a religion of the heart."

The new frontier in education is not a person's IQ but one's EQ—emotional quotient. Great leaders these days are judged not simply by their knowledge or vision but by their awareness of their own strengths and limitations, how well they understand their own feelings and manage them, and how well they can show empathy and connect with others.

Of course, the best leaders have always understood their emotions and known how to integrate them into their lives. Jesus gives us some classic examples.

One day he went to the home of a notorious tax collector named Zacchaeus. Through the course of the meal, Zacchaeus was convicted of his greed and converted to God. He stood up and said, "If I have cheated anyone," which he had, "I will pay them back four times over." The room fell stone silent. This couldn't be. People like him don't change. After the shock wore off, I can imagine his dinner guests cheering and applauding. Do you know what Jesus said?

> Today salvation has come to this house, because this man, too, is a son of Abraham.
>
> Luke 19:9 (NIV)

What were Zacchaeus and his guests feeling in that moment? **Joy!**

When Jesus came to the tomb of his close friend Lazarus, he saw Lazarus's sister Mary weeping along with many others. Scripture describes what happened next.

> Jesus wept.
>
> John 11:35 (NIV)

It's the shortest verse in the Bible, but these two words speak volumes about Jesus's emotional health. He wasn't afraid to openly express the deep **sadness** of loss.

When Jesus came to the temple in Jerusalem, he saw people who had traveled long distances to worship God. Greedy for gain, merchants charged these poor travelers outrageous prices for birds and other animals used for sacrifice. In a scene for the ages, Jesus overturned the tables of the money changers and drove them out with a whip, shouting:

> Is it not written: "My house will be called a house of prayer for all nations"? But you have made it "a den of robbers."
>
> Mark 11:17 (NIV)

The emotion on display for all was **anger**.

On a different day, Jesus was hungry:

> Seeing a fig tree by the road, he went up to it but found nothing on it except leaves. Then he said to it, "May you never bear fruit again!"
>
> Matthew 21:19 (NIV)

What emotion was that? **Disgust.**

In the garden of Gethsemane, just hours before he would die a horrific death on the cross, Jesus literally sweat blood as he begged with every ounce of his being:

> "Father," he said, "everything is possible for you. Take this cup from me."
>
> Mark 14:36 (NIV)

Understandably, what gripped his heart that night was **fear**.

Those who follow Christ believe that Jesus was not only fully God. He was also fully human. He experienced the full range of human emotions. By doing so, he set the pattern for us.

Transforming Practice: Listen to Your Emotions

In the midst of a fall, the fastest road to a comeback is listening to your emotions and integrating them into your life. Try these practical ways to tune in to your feelings.

Schedule Alone Time

Block off a morning, an afternoon, or an evening. If that seems like too much, make an appointment with yourself for one hour in a place free from interruptions. Retreat centers, libraries, and public parks are great for this kind of thing, but any quiet room away from others will do. When you arrive, shut down everything. No phone, no computer, no internet, no TV or radio, not even a book or magazine, nothing outside of a personal journal to write your reflections. Your goal is to disconnect, to slow down, and to let what is inside come up. Let yourself feel. To be honest, your first feeling may be guilt over "wasting" precious time. Don't be fooled. The value of this exercise is beyond estimation. Time alone is the single most powerful practice to reconnect with your true self.

Journal

If you struggle with your mind going in twenty-three directions at once (as I often do), a simple practice to slow your mind and focus your thoughts is journaling. Whether you pick up an inexpensive notebook, buy a specially designed journal, or start pounding away on a keyboard, the only requirement is to write down what is going on in you. Since I journal before going to bed at night, I often find it helpful to review my day, writing down the highs and lows, the places where God's presence was palpable, and those times when I felt alone or made mistakes. It's amazing what this basic practice can reveal. I have been journaling daily for many years now, and to be honest, sometimes I don't really know what I'm feeling until I start to write. It's like someone turned on a faucet, and what's deep inside comes pouring out.

As you become aware of your emotions, name them. When you say, "I'm feeling anxious," it takes you out of the state of anxiousness and gives you some control. Instead of being run by that emotion, you can now choose any of a hundred ways to handle it. One surprisingly effective option is to pray it.

Pray Your Feelings to God

Once you get a handle on the feelings swirling inside, you can talk to God about them. Author C. S. Lewis said, "We must lay before him what is in us; not what ought to be in us."[8] There is no need to be afraid. You are not going to surprise God. Just let what is inside come out. It may be messy. It may involve a tangled ball of anger, joy, disgust, fear, and shame. Just let it fly, unfiltered. God can handle it. Sometimes it helps to say it out loud. Maybe something like, "Lord, this what I'm feeling right now, and it doesn't make sense. I don't even know why. I'm mad. I'm sad. I'm scared. I'm at my wits' end! What are you trying to tell me through these feelings? Do I need to own something and apologize? Is there some truth you are trying to teach me? Or are you asking me to just sit still and feel it, so I can let it go?"

You may wonder, what real good could come from pouring out your jumbled emotional life before God? Alice Fryling explains it beautifully:

> The goal in focusing on our feelings is not to wallow in them. Nor is it just to clarify thinking. The goal is to notice and embrace the presence of God in this experience. When this happens, the peace that comes "transcends all understanding" (Philippians 4:7). In other words, we cannot think our way into God's peace; it's beyond our understanding. The Bible also says that the love of God "surpasses knowledge" (Ephesians 3:19). No matter how much we know, God's love is deeper, so sometimes the route to this peace beyond knowing is through our feelings.[9]

How many times have we missed the presence of God by focusing on what we know instead of laying out how we feel?

Not long ago, I talked with a young woman who saw the movie *Inside Out* just for fun, and it totally caught her off guard. At one point in the movie, she began to weep.

She, too, had moved as a little girl. Her family quickly dove into their new community, but it wasn't as easy for her. When she longed to go back, she was told to leave it behind and be happy in her new place.

She tried. She really did. But she missed her friends and her former life. She had lost a big part of her world and was never allowed to grieve it. Over time, stuffing her sadness resulted in physical illness.

Eventually, like the character Joy in the movie, she realized she didn't have to be happy all the time. The other emotions in her life were also crucial to her well-being. In a reflective moment, she shared, "I think I was creating a false sense of joy when I suppressed sadness. I thought it was happiness in the moment, but it couldn't have been because of how I was manipulating my feelings. It was when I allowed myself to actually sit in the sadness and 'feel' that true joy came out, because I felt free. Some of my deepest and most precious times with God have been a result of me learning to sit in the sadness with Him. It's very healing!"

Real faith is not something you do from the neck up. It never has been. We can't let emotions run our lives, or they will ruin them. But if we hide our emotions or run from them, it will lead to spiritual deadness. God created us with a full range of feelings. If we will listen to them, they can reveal a depth of love and a peace beyond understanding that only God can give.

Years ago, I ran across a prayer by Thomas Merton that's helped me in those times when I had fallen and didn't know which way to turn. If you find yourself there, try praying this as sincerely as you can:

> My Lord God,
>
> I have no idea where I am going. I do not see the road ahead of me. I cannot know for certain where it will end. Nor do I really know myself. And the fact that I think I am following your will does not mean that I am actually doing so.
>
> But I believe that the desire to please you does, in fact, please you. And I hope that I have that desire in all that I am doing. I hope that I will never do anything apart from that desire. And I know that if I do this you will lead me by the right road. Though I may know nothing about it.

> Therefore, I will trust you always. Though I may seem to be lost and in the shadow of death, I will not fear. For you are ever with me. And you will never leave me to face my perils alone.
>
> —Thomas Merton[10]

Sooner or later, everyone has a fall. It's terribly disorienting. The road ahead is unclear, and we don't know where it might lead. Naturally, that stirs a host of emotions. In that moment, we have a choice. We can intentionally ignore our feelings for fear they might slow us down or take us off track, or we can learn how to listen to our emotions without letting them control us. Feeling our feelings and listening to them sets us up for the next stage of the comeback journey.

Chapter 2

Coming to Yourself

Forward movement is not helpful if what is needed is a change of direction.

—David Fleming

I first met Jenny at church. She came one Sunday with three young children in tow. In our brief conversation after the service, she was pleasant but cautious. Her nine-year-old daughter showed no such reservation. She smiled and chatted as if she'd been there her whole life. Eager to please, she was the spitting image of her mother with long blonde hair pulled back in braids. Her younger brother and sister romped around like puppies finally let out of their cage. They joyfully pretended not to hear their mother's pleas to calm down.

Jenny continued to come on Sundays off and on, her kids always with her. After a while her husband showed up too, although he was clearly there under protest. An outdoors type who was good with his hands and sparing with his words, Jon listened intently but could think of a hundred other ways to spend his Sunday.

As their family felt more comfortable, I asked if I could stop by their house for a short visit to get to know them better. Jenny was hesitant, but the kids overruled her—loudly. I asked if I should call to set up a time. She said, "No, let's just pick a time now. We don't have a phone."

When I arrived late one afternoon, the kids jumped for joy over a visitor in the house. Jenny and I sat down at the kitchen table to talk while the kids buzzed in and out of the room showing off their favorite toy or recent drawing. Jon had just gotten off work and joined us a few minutes later.

The conversation started slowly. I could tell Jenny was nervous. Not many guests dropped by, and none of them had been a pastor. The house had seen better days. It was somewhere between a fixer-upper and a let-er goer. A variety of projects were in stages of repair along with various messes any parent with young children would recognize. None of that seemed to bother Jenny. Her tension centered on what came next.

After a brief chat about her kids and church, I asked where she grew up and what brought her to town. She looked down a lot, choosing her words carefully, until for some reason, the dam broke and her whole story came pouring out.

Jenny grew up in a nearby town in a hard-living family that barely made it by. Her mom became pregnant with her at sixteen and dropped out of school. Jenny never knew her father but had seen a parade of men in and out of her mother's life ever since she could remember. When Jenny turned sixteen, she, too, got pregnant and dropped out of school. The father of Jenny's first child left as soon as he heard the news. Her husband, Jon, came into the picture a few years later. Although he spent most nights at the local tap, at least he had a job. It was the most stable her life had ever been.

Casually, she added, "I don't really blame my mom. She did the best she could. After all, her mom got pregnant with her when she was sixteen and dropped out of school too."

At that moment, my heart broke for Jenny. Three generations of women became pregnant at sixteen, one right after the other. The day Jenny was born, her grandmother was thirty-two years old.

In a nanosecond, my entire perspective changed. Until then, I had assumed Jenny's childhood experience was similar to mine. I could not have been more wrong. Growing up in a stable, middle-class family with a mother and father who loved each other, loved their children, and gave them every opportunity, I was tempted to think Jenny wasn't trying hard enough. She didn't have to accept life the way it had been handed to her. Surely she could go back to school, get a job, and better herself.

Sadly, I had been viewing her life through the lens of my own. No wonder she had been so hesitant! I suddenly felt a level of compassion for Jenny, her husband, and her children I could not have dreamed possible. I wanted to marshal every resource imaginable to help them thrive.

That day I experienced a paradigm shift—a fundamental change in the way I saw the world. The word *paradigm* comes from the scientific community, but generally we use it to mean a person's perception, assumption, or worldview.

Twentieth-century scientist and philosopher Thomas Kuhn popularized the term *paradigm shift* by proposing that scientific fields do not progress in a smooth, linear fashion. Rather they experience "a series of peaceful interludes punctuated by intellectually violent revolutions." After these mental upheavals, Kuhn says, "one conceptual world view is replaced by another."[1] A classic example is Italian astronomer Galileo. When he first discovered the earth is not at the center of the universe but instead rotates around the sun, he unwittingly drew the ire of the Roman Catholic Church. Since his heliocentric model was contrary to official church teaching, Pope Urban VIII had him tried by the Inquisition and jailed for the charge of "vehemently suspect of heresy."

Both scientific and religious thought leaders of the day were strongly attached to the old paradigm of a geocentric universe. Their stalwart belief that the sun revolves around the earth led them to fervently discredit Galileo at every turn.

Of course, today we know Galileo was right, but it took a long time to get there. Through the 1700s, schools taught both orbital models. Eventually, astronomers amassed enough data to win the day.

Although the College of Cardinals finally allowed books to be published with the heliocentric model in 1822, you may wonder how long it took the Vatican to exonerate Galileo.

The church first attacked Galileo in 1633. In 1992, the *New York Times* reported on a thirteen-year Vatican review of Galileo's case. In the end, Pope John Paul II admitted the church had wrongly imprisoned him over 350 years later![2]

Clearly, worldviews die harder than Bruce Willis. They exert such a powerful hold because they provide our frame of reference for all our life decisions. Imagine how different Jenny's life might have been if given a different paradigm by her mother and grandmother. She quietly whispered to me her hope that her oldest daughter would take a different path.

Paradigms are literally the way we understand the world, so no one wants to admit being wrong. It could lead to a violent internal revolution. The pressure to hold our paradigms in place and keep our cognitive peace is enormous.

At the same time, a paradigm shift offers an opportunity for immense change in our lives. Whenever we experience a fundamental shift in thinking, as I did in my conversation with Jenny or as the world did with Galileo's discovery, our lives are suddenly placed in a whole new orbit. We see ourselves and the world in a more accurate light—one that aligns more closely to reality.

However, massive shifts are not our preferred means of change. Philosopher Ken Wilbur says most of us are only willing to question 5 percent of what we know at any one time.[3] When it comes to improving our lives, most of us stick to minor, incremental change by focusing on our attitude and behavior. Of course, this approach assumes we are seeing the world as it really is, which may or may not be true. Our paradigm is like a map of a city. If you are in Chicago and all you have is a map of Dallas, it doesn't matter how positive your attitude or how hard you try to reach your destination, you will still be lost. A focus on attitude and behavior only helps when you have the right map.[4] Even then, our best hope is incremental change. On the other hand, awe-inspiring, large-scale change happens when we focus on our paradigms.

Stephen Covey describes the difference using this famous quotation.

> In the words of Thoreau, "For every thousand hacking at the leaves of evil, there is one striking at the root." We can only achieve quantum improvements in our lives as we quit hacking at the leaves of

> attitude and behavior and get to work on the root, the paradigms from which our attitudes and behaviors flow.[5]

In Jesus's story about the prodigal son, the younger son was struggling with his map. He had brashly demanded his share of the inheritance from his father and set off to a far country to live the life of his dreams.

Life as a high roller was pretty enticing for a while. It was party time all the time. But when the money ran out, he found himself in a far country with a map that didn't work. To make matters worse, a severe famine hit the land. To keep from starving, the young man found menial work feeding pigs. He was so hungry, he even considered eating the pods he threw to the pigs. But to his surprise, no one gave him anything.

As his stomach rumbled, something happened to the younger son for the very first time:

> He began to be in need.
>
> Luke 15:14 (NRSV)

It signaled the beginning of something new. Before a profound shift can occur in our life, we must come to an awareness of our need.

Real change is need driven. If we don't feel any need, we won't make any changes. This explains why genuine faith is so hard for independent, self-made people. "We're doing just fine on our own. Thank you very much." But sooner or later, life breaks through our illusion of self-sufficiency, and suffering shows up at our doorstep. It may be the loss of a loved one or the loss of a job, a broken relationship or a bankruptcy, a heart attack or a prison sentence. Whatever the specifics, the tragic nature of life touches us—painfully. We sadly discover we are not immune after all. No one is. Losing, failing, and falling is a part of every life. And even though no right-minded person would willingly choose it, a fall offers a gift we desperately need. It ushers us into reality.

A quirk of human nature is some tragedy must occur for the autopilot mode of everyday life to click off. Dire losses grab us by the collar and hold up a mirror in front of us. They show us our lives as they really are. Without them, our true condition remains buried under the layers of an ever-successful, always-in-control false self. Unexpected falls serve a sober and essential purpose. They give us eyes to see our glaring limits and our acute need. No significant change will occur until that point.

As the younger son stood alone in the field with oinking pigs, his gnawing need led to a turning point. Jesus says,

> But when he came to himself . . .
>
> Luke 15:17 (NRSV)

There, in a flash of insight, reality broke through. The younger son finally stepped outside of his life just far enough to look back and see it as it really was. He said to himself, "How many of my father's hired hands have more than enough food, but I'm starving to death!"[6]

At that moment, his paradigm shifted. His need led him to the truth about himself. He was starving because of his own mistakes and his own pride, and he didn't have to live that way anymore.

My friends Dave and Cindy understand how a need can pierce the veneer of self-sufficiency and bring a shift in worldview. Dave tells their story this way:

> My wife and I were married thirty-five years ago and have been on a lifetime roller-coaster ride. When we married, we both had ambitions of traveling places, having a nice home, raising our children together as a family of six (we both had two children from previous marriages), own nice cars, and improve financially each year. We both worked outside the home. I took pride in getting bonuses and winning trips to fantastic destinations each year.
>
> Five years into our marriage we learned our youngest, Ann, had a slow-developing, terminal illness. It was devastating news, but we both were raised to "suck it up" and use our own strength to move forward—and that's what we did.
>
> After living in the same area for fourteen years, I received a promotion to a regional manager position that required us to move. It included a large bonus, increase in salary, expense account, company credit card, and new company vehicle each year, not to mention the trips. I didn't know how it could get any better! Now I could get my wife a new luxury car and a new home in a gated area. We were living the "American Dream."
>
> As we settled into our new home, another dark cloud appeared on the horizon. One of my customers was an avid deer hunter, and I would go hunting with him every November. Without warning, he had a massive heart attack in his sleep and died. He was my age and left behind a wife and two young boys. I thought, "What now? What purpose did he or any of us have on earth?" I was a pallbearer at a very

somber funeral. As we left the cemetery, my head was full of unanswered questions.

Until then, God and church never figured into our equation. I had gone to church as a child with my parents and mainly looked at it as getting a cherry coke and a burger after the service. My wife had only attended church occasionally with her friends. As adults we didn't think about church much because we had everything "under control."

Not long after, we noticed a new church being built on the west side of our city and thought maybe we should check it out. When we finally walked in one Sunday, people greeted us like they really cared. We felt like we were "home"! It was truly an awakening because inside we were searching for something more.

That September, the church began a weekly series on the purpose of life. We were so interested in the topic, we signed up to meet with a small group of people in someone's home for six weeks. In our group, we learned that God had a purpose for us while we were on earth. We both bought our first Bibles and started reading the Gospel of John. Amazingly, it became enjoyable to go to church and be involved with the people.

Months later, on December 18 of that year, I received a phone call from my corporate headquarters requesting that I attend a meeting the next day at 9:00 a.m. I thought to myself, "That's awfully short notice." But I prepared to leave the next morning. When I arrived, I was summoned to a conference room where I was met by three corporate employees I had never seen. One woman had a stack of papers four to five

> inches thick. She said, "We have called you here to review your expense reports for the last year and a half."
>
> One by one she pointed out discrepancies in the reports and asked for explanations of each. I didn't have any. After three hours she said, "We are terminating your employment effective tomorrow. We will pick up your vehicle, laptop, printer, fax, and any other company property, plus the bill for several thousand dollars owed."
>
> Humiliated and ashamed, I got back in my truck, called my wife, and told her I had been fired. What hurt the most was my wife knew nothing about my misuse of company funds over fifteen years with that company.
>
> When I finally got home, my wife and I just held each other, weeping. She needed an explanation. I didn't know what to say.
>
> On December 22 at 11:00 a.m., we met with our pastor, told him what happened, and surrendered control of our lives to Jesus Christ. We realized God wanted us, and the only way God could reach me was by taking away what I held onto the hardest—my job!

Talk about a paradigm shift. When they came to themselves, Dave and Cindy's entire orbit changed. They were no longer at the center of the universe with all things revolving around them. Now their lives were revolving around a new center, Jesus Christ. Their hidden need to find something more than material success and their aching need for redemption led them to a wholesale change of their worldview. They replaced their American dream with God's dream for them. As a result, they discovered a much larger purpose for their lives. More on that later.

Perhaps the greatest worldview shift in the Bible occurred to a man named Saul—one of the most zealous religious men of his day. Saul was a Jewish leader, a Pharisee, someone who strictly adhered to the 613 laws in the Hebrew Bible (what Christians call the Old Testament). Saul became known for violently opposing an upstart movement called The Way. He came by that reputation honestly.

In the earliest days of the church, just a couple of months after Jesus was crucified, an early follower of Jesus named Stephen enraged the Jewish elders of Jerusalem by claiming Jesus had been raised from the dead. They immediately dragged him out of the city and threw stones at him to kill him. As this scene played out, the elders laid their coats at the feet of a young man named Saul. Luke, another early disciple and eyewitness to this execution, writes these chilling words:

> And Saul approved of their killing him.
>
> Acts 8:1 (NRSV)

That began a massive persecution of the early church, and Saul became a brutal ringleader. People scattered from Jerusalem to the countryside to save their lives.

Saul didn't care if they ran. He ravaged little bands of believers wherever they hid. He would enter house after house and drag off both men and women to throw them into prison.

While "breathing threats and murder against the disciples of the Lord,"[7] Saul went to the Jewish high priest in Jerusalem and asked for letters to the synagogues at Damascus. If Saul found any followers of The Way who had scattered north, men or women, he would bind them in shackles and bring them back to Jerusalem for likely execution.

On his approach to Damascus, a sudden light from heaven shined on him. He immediately fell to the ground and heard a voice say, "Saul, Saul, why do you persecute me?"

Saul had no idea what was going on. "Who are you, Lord?" he asked.

"I am Jesus, whom you are persecuting," he replied.

What?! Saul didn't think for a minute he was persecuting some folk rabbi from Galilee who had been crucified by the Romans.

The voice continued, "Now get up and go into the city, and you will be told what you must do."[8] When Saul got up, his eyes were open, but he couldn't see. The men traveling with him had to lead him by the hand into Damascus. Blind and baffled, Saul refused to eat or drink for three days.

Now comes the really wild part. In Damascus, there was a disciple named Ananias, probably one of the believers who scattered from Jerusalem. Jesus appeared to him in a vision and said, "Ananias, go to Straight street, at the house of Judas and look for a man named Saul. He's praying right now, and he has seen a man named Ananias come and lay hands on him to restore his sight."

Now, pause it right there and put yourself in Ananias's sandals. Would you be excited about this assignment? Uh, no! Neither was he. In fact, he argues with Jesus: "Lord, I don't think this is such a good idea. I'm not sure if you know this, but this guy has done a lot of evil stuff to your people in Jerusalem. And he's come here to take out your followers! If it's OK with you, Lord, I think I'll just sit this one out."

> But the Lord said to Ananias, "Go! This man is my chosen instrument to proclaim my name to the Gentiles and their kings and to the people of Israel."
>
> Acts 9:15 (NIV)

Ananias must have been saying under his breath, "Are we talking about the same guy? I don't think he's the instrument-of-God type?"

In spite of his apprehension, Ananias did what Jesus said even when it didn't make sense. Arriving at Judas's house, Ananias laid his hands on Saul and said, "Brother Saul, the Lord—Jesus, who appeared to you on the road as you were coming here—has sent me so that you may see again and be filled with the Holy Spirit."[9]

Instantly, Saul could see again. He got up, was baptized, and took some food. After several days with the other disciples in Damascus, Saul began to stand up in the synagogues and proclaim, "Jesus is the Son of God."

Wait. Seriously?! A couple of weeks before, he wrapped people in chains and threw them in prison for saying that stuff. Notice the pattern? Saul was charging along on his own mission, and suddenly, he found himself in need. The supposedly dead founder of the movement he was persecuting put him in a three-day timeout. With eyes that couldn't see and a mind that couldn't comprehend, Saul had a lot of time to think and pray.

When Ananias risked his life to pray for him, you hear the most poignant description of a paradigm shift in all of Scripture:

> Immediately, something like scales fell from Saul's eyes, and he could see again.
>
> Acts 9:18 (NIV)

When he came to himself, Saul's first act was to get baptized as a follower of Jesus. Here again, we see the entire orbit of someone's life change. Instead of revolving around the Jewish Law as the center of his universe, Saul put Jesus Christ at the center. Saul goes from persecutor to proclaimer of Christ. So profound was this change that Saul spent the remainder of his life planting churches across the Roman Empire and was executed for his faith. The letters he wrote to those early Christian communities later became the lion's share of the New Testament of the Bible. Most know him better by his Roman name, Paul.

Saul, Galileo, and Dave and Cindy all experienced a fundamental change in the way they saw the world. Note the common threads that run through their stories:

- Paradigms are very powerful.
- Whether accurate or not, our paradigms provide the basis for all our life's decisions.
- Paradigms don't change quickly or easily.
- When a paradigm shifts, it causes great upheaval for a time.
- The first sign of real change is when a need breaks through our illusion of self-sufficiency.
- Paradigms shift when we step outside of our lives just far enough to look back and see life as it really is.

Let's assume for the moment that these statements are true. For a comeback of any kind to occur, we must first listen to our emotions and become aware of a real need. It may be physical like the younger son's hunger, emotional like Dave and Cindy's need for redemption, or spiritual like Saul's encounter on the road to Damascus. Our need leads us to reexamine our mental maps, see assumptions that may be holding us in the wrong orbit, and open our minds to changing them. All this takes place when we engage in an unfamiliar practice to most people—solitude.

Transforming Practice: Choose Solitude and Stillness

Solitude is a time when we withdraw from others to be alone with God.

You may be thinking, "Right. Who's got time for that?" Even the concept is foreign to us. Solitude flies in the face of our frenetic lives. It's completely out of step with our 24/7 culture. There's just so much that has to be done.

Trust me, I'm with you.

Let me share a confession. I am busy. At first blush, that may not sound so bad, but over time, I've discovered the insidiousness of this sin.

On the surface, busyness appears as a virtue. People say, "Look at the progress we've made and the people we've touched. All our charts are up and to the right. This is fantastic!" And it is. It's also a great way to get noticed and affirmed. I just didn't know how easy it would be to lose my soul.

I'm not talking here about busyness interspersed with rest and play. I'm referring to head down, nose to the grindstone, morning, noon, and night busyness in both paid and unpaid work. The kind that goes on for weeks and months, maybe years. It's relentless busyness that hardens your heart, shrivels your relationships, narrows your perspective, and makes it almost impossible to hear the voice of God. I know. I've been there.

Ironically, this is not the life Jesus modeled. Of course, Jesus had many things to do. He had people to heal, disciples to mentor, and crowds to teach. But he was never in a hurry. When word reached Jesus that his friend Lazarus was ill, he didn't rush off to his side. Instead, Jesus stayed two days longer where he was (John 11:5-6). Somehow, Jesus was just fine with moving slowly. Why aren't we?

Author Eugene Peterson offers two revealing insights:

> *I am busy because I am vain.* I want to appear important. Significant. What better way than to be busy? The incredible hours, the crowded schedule, and the heavy demands on my time are proof to myself—and to all who will notice—that I am important. If I go into a doctor's office and find there's no one waiting, and I see through a half-open door the doctor reading a book, I wonder if he's any good. . . .
>
> Such experiences affect me. I live in a society in which crowded schedules and harassed conditions are evidence of importance, so I develop a crowded schedule and harassed conditions. When others notice, they acknowledge my significance, and my vanity is fed.
>
> *I am busy because I am lazy.* I indolently let others decide what I will do instead of resolutely deciding myself. It was a favorite theme of C. S. Lewis that only lazy people work hard. By lazily abdicating the essential work of deciding and directing, establishing values and setting goals, other people do it for us.[10]

If you are like me, this hits a little too close to home. I used to think busyness was thrust on me by my job or stage of life. I know better now. Regardless of where I live, the kind of work I do, or my season of life, I find ways to pack my schedule. It's no one else's fault. It's something in me.

Meyer Friedman, who pioneered studies in type A behavior, gives a definition of what some call "hurry sickness." He describes hurry sickness as "above all a continuous struggle and unremitting attempt to accomplish or achieve more and more things or participate in more and more events in less and less time, frequently in the face of opposition, real or imagined, from other persons."[11]

If you or someone you know is acquainted with this disease, there is hope. Solitude and stillness are the antidote to hurry sickness. If we will set aside time to draw away from others to be alone with God, this spiritual sickness can be healed.

The practice is very simple.

1. **Set aside some time alone each day.** It's easiest if you set the same time every day. That way you can build it into your schedule as a habit.

2. **Find a quiet place apart from interruptions.** Anything with an "on" button needs to be turned off. If possible, go to the same place each day.

3. **Find a comfortable position.** Feel free to stand, sit, or kneel. You may prefer a solitary walk in nature.

4. **As you begin, notice your breathing.** Put yourself in tune with the rhythms of your body. Take some deep breaths. Relax.

5. **Release any worries or concerns.** You may put your palms down and symbolically let them go.

6. **Receive.** Listen quietly for the messages your body, your emotions, your spirit, and God have to say. You may put your palms up as a sign of receiving.

If you have never done this kind of thing before, start small. Occasional joggers do not run marathons. Take five to ten minutes each day. One businessman told me he started coming into his office ten minutes earlier. He made some coffee and sat there all by himself just to listen. He was amazed by what he began to hear when he created some space for God to speak. You, too, will be amazed at all the messages that were trying to get through, but the line was always busy.

A reality I am slowly beginning to own is that you can't change a tire going ninety miles an hour. If you want to change a tire, you have to stop the car. Scripture puts it this way,

> Be still, and know that I am God!
>
> Psalm 46:10 (NRSV)

God is known in stillness. Notice this passage doesn't say, "Do still." It's not about our accomplishments. In solitude, we are not trying to earn God's praise; we are trying to enter God's presence. Some say, "80 percent of life is showing up." In God's view, "100 percent of solitude is showing up." It's simply withdrawing from others to be alone with God. You cannot fail at this. Don't worry about whether God is doing anything or whether you are doing anything. This is not a "do" thing. This is a "be" thing. It is enough just to be in the presence of an all-powerful and all-loving God.

When we regularly take time to withdraw from others to be alone with God, a number of gifts become available that can significantly change our lives. I will mention just three.

Solitude Reveals Who I Am

Solitude affords us the breathing room to let our lives speak. Who we are and who we were made to be is in us, but our ceaseless stream of activity muffles the inner voice of our true calling. Parker Palmer describes the struggle we all face to embrace our unique purpose in life:

> Vocation does not come from a voice "out there" calling me to become something I am not. It comes from a voice "in here" calling me to be the person I was born to be, to fulfill the original selfhood given me at birth by God.
>
> It is a strange gift, this birthright of self. Accepting it turns out to be even more demanding than attempting to become someone else! . . . There is a Hasidic tale that reveals . . . both the universal tendency to want to be somebody else and the ultimate importance of becoming one's self. Rabbi Zusya, when he was an old man said, "In the coming world, they will not ask me: 'Why were you not Moses?' They will ask me: 'Why were you not Zusya?'"[12]

Being precedes doing. What we do arises from who we are. As we take time to sit in stillness, who we are and are meant to be slowly rise to the surface.

Solitude Reveals the True Needs of My Heart

Email, meetings, phone calls, family needs, classes, games, meetings, work, homework, travel, projects, doctor's appointments, practice, email, errands, concerts, meetings, sporting events, reports, household chores, and on and on. It makes me tired just listing them. No wonder we spend so little time in solitude. And no wonder we're unaware of our true needs. They get buried in busyness!

Here's how I've tried to unearth them. For many years, I have made it a practice to take a few days up to two weeks for a "study break" in the summer. It's a time to disconnect from my normal world to more fully connect with God. It works best for me to leave town and find a place filled with the beauty of nature. Each time, without fail, God reveals to me the true needs of my heart: the places that need healing, the places that need encouragement, the places that need comfort, the places that need to be challenged. Several times I've discovered something I was still grieving but didn't know it. I had simply covered up the loss with work and busyness, but it was still there, waiting to receive consolation and peace.

As I've gotten better at this discipline, I've realized I don't have to wait a whole year for the Holy Spirit to do this work. As I spend more dedicated time alone in the mornings, God reveals to me the places where I'm afraid, sad, grateful, or angry—where I need to be bold and where I need to be gentle. Without solitude, none of these insights would be available to me, but all of the feelings and needs they reveal would still be stirring inside. Now, instead of those needs unconsciously driving my life, I can name them and choose how to address them. That's the gift of solitude and stillness.

Solitude Gives Me a New Perspective on My Life

Once the true needs of our hearts are revealed, they can lead us to reexamine our mental maps. Notice the common thread in each of the three paradigm-shift stories shared earlier. Before the shift occurred, all of these people spent significant time alone. The younger son was feeding pigs out in a field by himself. Dave and Cindy spent time reading their new Bibles and considering their true purpose in life. Saul spent three days alone without sight, food, or water. In those still times, God was preparing them for a fundamental shift in the way they saw the world.

In each case, they came to a startling new realization. It was their own fault. They were where they were due to their own choices and mistakes. No one else was to blame. This single shift in perspective, born in solitude, changed everything.

Often our assumptions trap us in a negative orbit. We fall prey to a victim mindset that finds fault in everyone and everything but us.

We say, "I can't help it, the car wouldn't start, my coworker shredded it, my dog got sick, my family is a mess, my husband forgot, my girlfriend is psycho, my boss is bizarre," and on it goes.

By blaming others and our circumstances, we give away our power to people and things outside us. We lose our agency. We become small.

Of course, sometimes things happen to us that really are beyond our control, but we can still choose how we will respond to them. We have response-ability. One of the most practical, paradigm-shifting truths I have ever heard came from Stephen Covey: *"Anytime we think the problem is 'out there,' that thought is the problem."*[13]

Blaming is a self-defeating behavior that keeps us stuck in old paradigms. We can choose a different response to the things that happen to us. We can choose acceptance. Acceptance is the ability to accept life exactly as it is for the moment.

Instead of resisting reality and saying, "I don't want to be fired," "I don't want a life-threatening illness," "I don't want to be divorced," or "I don't want to have an addiction," we can use our response-ability. We can stare reality in the eye and say, "Yes, this is where I am. I don't like it. I don't want to be here, but the problem is not 'out there.' It's 'in here.' Can I accept this situation as it is deep within myself?" Once we make that shift, our lives can change for the better. I like the way Melody Beattie puts it: "For anything to change or anyone to change, we must first accept ourselves, others, and the circumstance exactly as they are."[14]

It is a paradox. Until we accept where we are, we are chained to a reality we do not want. Now, add the miracle of faith, and say, "This is exactly where I am supposed to be right now."[15] I need to be here, so I can continue on the path God has laid out for me.

This changes everything, and it opens us to the guidance we will need to continue the journey.

Chapter 3

The Gift of Guidance

Fools see their own way as right,
but the wise listen to advice.

—Proverbs 12:15 (CEB)

It was a week after New Year's, and I had come to football saturation point. After watching little known teams duke it out in various "Rental Car" Bowls, I really wasn't that interested in a game between some Ducks and Horned Frogs.

My son turned it on and promptly left to hang out with friends. As I did some things around the house, I came in and out of the family room, casually checking the score. It wasn't much of a game. By halftime, the Oregon Ducks were up 31–0. I almost turned it off but got involved with other things.

When I came back in the third quarter, Texas Christian University had just put some points on the board. It was 31–10 at that point. On the kick return, Oregon fumbled the ball deep in their own territory. The Horned Frogs recovered and promptly scored. It was now 31–17. I thought, "This is turning into a game, but Oregon is still going to win."

At that point, I was tired and wanted to be fresh for Sunday morning, so I turned off the TV and went to bed. Wouldn't you know, when I got to church the next morning, someone said, "Did you see that TCU game?" I said, "Part of it. Why?"

"Well, they were down 31–0 at halftime, and they came back in the second half to tie it. In the *third* overtime, they won!"

"*Seriously*?!" Sure enough, the TCU Horned Frogs won the 2016 Alamo Bowl 47–41. It tied the record for the biggest comeback in college bowl history. (I *knew* I should have stayed up to watch that game!)

Ever noticed how much people enjoy telling a story like that? They start out describing how bleak the situation had become. Just when you're agreeing with them that it's a lost cause, a ray of hope enters the picture. What seems impossible moves to improbable, and suddenly the entire situation is reversed! The closer people get to the climax of the story, the louder their voice, the wider their smile, and the greater their wonder over the magic of it all.

Stories like this are immensely popular in our culture perhaps because, somewhere along the line, we've all had a failure or two. We made a mistake. We let someone down. We got behind in the first half, and we needed a comeback of our own, a chance to be redeemed.

There may be no one who needed a bigger comeback than King David in the Bible. He was a shepherd boy God had specifically chosen to be the leader of his people, Israel. David was a deeply spiritual man. He wrote most of the psalms in the Old Testament of the Bible. The psalms are songs and prayers to God about all the changing circumstances of life. They are beautiful and raw and heartfelt, obviously written by someone who had a close relationship with God.

Yet this godly man made some very ungodly choices that caused great harm. You find the story in the Old Testament book of 2 Samuel. Here's the setup:

> In the spring of the year, the time when kings go out to battle, David sent Joab with his officers and all Israel with him; they ravaged the Ammonites, and besieged Rabbah. But David remained at Jerusalem.
>
> It happened, late one afternoon, when David rose from his couch and was walking about on the roof of the king's house, that he saw from the roof a woman bathing; the woman was very beautiful. David sent someone to inquire about the woman. It was reported, "This is Bathsheba daughter of Eliam, the wife of Uriah the Hittite." So David sent messengers to get her, and she came to him, and he lay with her. . . . Then she returned to her house. The woman conceived; and she sent and told David, "I am pregnant."
>
> 2 Samuel 11:1-5 (NRSV)

These words stopped David cold. He thought, as king, he could have this little fling with Bathsheba, and no one would be the wiser. But she became pregnant, and everyone knew her husband was off fighting in one of David's wars.

Now he faced a choice: come clean or cover up. If it happened today, political advisors would say, "Just come clean. Own up. It will be bad publicity for a while, but people will get over it. Your poll numbers are good. This will be a little bump in the road."

But this was ancient Israel. When David heard the words, "I am pregnant," he knew what that meant. The Law prescribed the death penalty for both David and Bathsheba.

David was now at a crossroads. His sin had put two innocent lives at stake, that of Bathsheba and their unborn child, so he opted for a cover-up. He sent for Bathsheba's husband, Uriah, who was fighting on the front line.

When Uriah returned to Jerusalem, the king asked about the troops and how the war was going. Wryly he said, "Go down to your house, wash your feet, relax."

David sent a gift basket of food, so Uriah and his wife could have a happy reunion. But Uriah slept at the entrance to the palace and didn't go down to his house that night.

When David found out the next day, he questioned Uriah. His foot soldier explained, "My commander Joab and my lord's men are camped in the open country. How could I go to my house to eat and drink and make love to my wife? As surely as you live, I will not do such a thing!"[1]

Who knew this man would be so loyal and full of character? David had to shift to plan B. The next day he invited Uriah to dine with him at the king's table, and David got him drunk. But that night, Uriah again slept on his mat among the king's servants. He didn't go home.

The following day, David's plans took a darker turn. He wrote a letter to Joab, the commander of his army, and sent it with Uriah. It said,

> Set Uriah in the forefront of the hardest fighting, and then draw back from him, so that he may be struck down and die.
>
> 2 Samuel 11:15 (NRSV)

Joab followed the king's orders without delay. In the midst of heavy fighting, the army pulled back. Several of Israel's soldiers were killed, including Uriah the Hittite.

When word reached Jerusalem, Bathsheba mourned the death of her husband. After the time of mourning was over—probably seven days—David brought her to his house. She soon became his wife and bore him a son.

The plan worked. David had saved Bathsheba, their son, and himself. No one ever had to know.

Except someone did know. The last line of chapter 11 reads:

> But the thing that David had done displeased the LORD.
>
> 2 Samuel 11:27 (NRSV)

Unbeknownst to him, David had set in motion a fall of epic proportions. Sometimes you experience a fall because you make an honest mistake. You thought the light was green when it was red, and you have a fender bender. You inadvertently flip a couple of numbers in the annual report, and it throws off the rest of the figures.

One time in college, I studied ridiculously hard for a test that was set for 6:30 at night. By 6:00, I felt I was ready. It was about a ten-minute walk to the exam hall from my dorm room, so I laid down for a moment to rest my mind. When I woke up, it was 6:29. People still wonder about that streak that shot through campus that night. Needless to say, I didn't do quite as well on that test. When incidents like these happen, you feel bad about it, but you didn't do it on purpose. It's best to just learn from it and move on.

At other times we fall because we knowingly make a bad choice, or maybe a string of bad choices, like David.

Then what? How do you come back when you knew it was wrong, but you did it anyway?

First, let's put it in the context of the larger journey. We know that sooner or later, everyone has a fall. When that happens, our best course of action is to listen to our emotions. A healthy awareness of what is really going on inside keeps us from getting stuck or allowing unidentified emotions to take us down deeper.

The second stage in our comeback journey is to come to ourselves. We need a shift in our perspective that enables us to understand the real problem and our part in it. At this point in David's life, that shift hasn't happened. He thinks he has outwitted the demands of the Law and outplayed the other characters in this drama. He has taken what he wanted and left all consequences in the rearview mirror. It's good to be the king.

But the Lord sees the situation differently. God sends the prophet Nathan to David with a story. Nathan tells of two men, one rich and one poor. The rich man had sheep and cattle galore, but the poor man had just one little lamb. He raised it like his own child, sharing his food and drink with it and letting it sleep in his arms.

One day a traveler showed up at the rich man's door. The rich man refused to take one of his own sheep or cattle to prepare a meal for the traveler. Instead, he took the one little lamb that belonged to the poor man and prepared it for his traveling guest.

As David heard the story, he seethed with righteous anger. "As surely as the LORD lives, the man who did this must die!"[2]

> Then Nathan said to David, "You are the man!"
>
> 2 Samuel 12:7 (NIV)

Suddenly, a shift occurred. David saw himself for who he was—a rich man who shamelessly took a poor man's one little lamb for himself.

Consider the irony when someone shouts at a sports event, "You 'da man!" When Nathan used this phrase, it wasn't a compliment. It was a conviction.

Nathan told him the Lord saw the whole sordid story, and it grieved God's heart. By his evil actions, David had "despised" the Lord, and there would be severe consequences.[3]

It was a tense moment. If David was offended by Nathan exposing this dark secret, he would have Nathan's head. But when the truth came out, instead of denying it or attacking the messenger, David confessed it.

> I have sinned against the Lord.
>
> 2 Samuel 12:13 (NRSV)

Let's pull back for a moment and take in the wide angle. Left to himself, David would have buried this wicked account of adultery, murder, and deception. It came to light and eventually became an instrument of transformation in his life for one reason: *he listened to wise counsel.*

Transforming Practice: Seek Wise Counsel

Seeking wise counsel is a breakout practice for anyone who really wants to come back. In fact, it's a crucial part of what mythologists and storytellers the world over call the "Hero's Journey." You may have noticed that seeking out a guide is a basic plot point in nearly every novel, movie, play, or musical you know. It's so common in popular movies, we don't give it much thought.

- *Rocky:* Rocky Balboa is trained by Mickey.
- *Star Wars:* Luke Skywalker is tutored by Obi-Wan Kenobi.
- *The Hunger Games:* Katniss relies on Haymitch.

- *The Lord of the Rings:* Frodo seeks out Gandalf.
- *Frozen:* Elsa and Anna consult Grand Pabbie (the Troll King).

In each case, the hero is unable to overcome his or her problem and take action without the wise counsel of a guide. It's a necessary part of the plot. It's also a necessary part of life.

We are all on a transformation journey. We wake up every morning as the hero of our story. Yet all of us have made mistakes (some accidentally, some knowingly), and we all need help to come back. We intuitively know if we could solve our own problems, we wouldn't have fallen in the first place. We need a guide, someone who understands our plight and helps us overcome our fear.[4]

All of us have relied on a guide at different points in our lives: our mother or father who patiently loved us through a rebellious stage, a teacher who sparked a love for reading or music or math, a coach who showed us the power of teamwork to accomplish a big goal, or a mentor who helped us see a larger purpose for our lives.

Perhaps because I am often so clueless, I've been blessed with many excellent guides. But one, in particular, wasn't even on my radar. It was about a year after I completed my ministry studies. I was serving as an associate pastor in Moline, Illinois, when I realized something was missing. My responsibilities at the church were going well. I had good friends. Family was good. But I felt dry. Dry on the inside. It finally dawned on me that I needed a deeper connection with God.

Almost by accident, I heard someone talk about spiritual direction. It was described as meeting with a spiritual coach who helps you identify what God is up to in your life and follow the Spirit's leading.

The whole idea intrigued me. I knew I needed help, so I looked up a recommended place, set up an appointment, and showed up with wobbly hope. I found myself sitting across from a man about twenty years my senior named Bill Creed—Father Bill Creed. He was a Jesuit Priest. The same order as Pope Francis.

That first session lasted about forty-five minutes. It was mostly getting to know each other, and frankly, it underwhelmed me. In fact, I almost didn't go back. But I was dry. Dry on the inside. And I needed help if I hoped to stay in the ministry.

Three weeks later, I showed up for a second session, and it blew me away. Father Bill identified exactly what was going on inside me and gave great suggestions on how to move forward. That was in 1987. I've been talking with him ever since.

Over time I came to realize this was the most spiritual man I had ever met. He had a gift for discerning the spiritual core beneath my surface slush and bringing it into the light.

It would be impossible for me to overstate the role he has played in my life. He was one of three people who laid hands on me at my ordination (and reminds me I'm one-third Jesuit). He was one of the pastors who officiated my wedding. He's taught me how to listen for God, how to be in God's presence, and how to wrestle with God through difficult times. To be honest, he's kept my train from going off the tracks more times than I could count. Even though there are stretches when we don't talk for months, I keep coming back for one reason. Somehow, through this man I hear the voice of God. I don't want to give that up.

Who is your guide? The recovery community has a saying, "When you are inside your own head, you're behind enemy lines."

We need people who can draw us out of ourselves. There is a passage in the Bible that describes why this is so important.

> The human heart is the most deceitful of all things,
> and desperately wicked.
>
> Jeremiah 17:9 (NLT)

What does that mean? We know we're capable of deceiving others. We sometimes try to deceive God. But more than that, we can deceive ourselves without even knowing it. We have deluxe rationalizers between our ears. We can turn white into black and black white if it's to our advantage. That's why we need people who will help us see things in our lives and in the world as they really are, not as we think they are or wish they were. Trusted friends or family members, a mentor, a pastor, a certified coach, or a skilled counselor can help us get in touch with reality, deal with our feelings about it, and choose how to move forward.

Among other things, a wise guide reveals the blind spots that trip us up. Back in 1955, psychologists Joseph Luft and Harrington Ingham created a four-paned diagram to help us understand the multi-dimensional relationship we have with ourselves and others. They called it the Johari window.

The upper left pane is known as the Open area or Arena. It is the part of ourselves that is known both to others and to us. It includes information, facts, skills, and attitudes—anything we choose to communicate to others.

The bottom left pane is the Hidden area. These are thoughts, feelings, opinions, and experiences known only to us, which we choose to keep private.

The top right pane is our Blind Spot. Here's where others know things about us that we do not. These things could be pos-

	Known by Self	Unknown by Self
Known to Others	Open	Blind Spot
Unknown to Others	Hidden	Unknown to all

itive or negative and include hidden strengths or areas for improvement. A guide can be a *huge* help in moving strengths and weaknesses in this pane into the Open pane.

The bottom right pane is Unknown. It includes information, skills, behaviors, and even feelings that are unknown both to us and to others. It could include subconscious information such as early childhood memories or undiscovered talents.[5]

In addition to revealing blind spots, a skilled guide may also lure treasures out of this Unknown area. Three thousand years ago, wise King Solomon wrote:

> A person's thoughts are like water in a deep well,
> but someone with insight can draw them out.
>
> Proverbs 20:5 (GNT)

The longer I cling to this planet, the more I realize how much of myself is unknown to me on any given day. The old adage "What you don't know can't hurt you" couldn't be further from the truth. More often than not, what lurks below our conscious awareness is what drives our most destructive behaviors. To come back from a fall, we need someone with insight who can draw out the deep stuff.

In some ways, our struggle is like swimming along an ocean shoreline. My wife and I like to snorkel and recently went to a beautiful site in the Pacific. Before we jumped in, those who had just returned warned us of the waves out on the point. The open sea rolls into the point with massive force. Unsuspecting snorkelers can be so dazzled by the underwater beauty, they swim too close to shore and get caught by the waves as they crash onto the rocks. Part of the reason it's so difficult to escape is the dual nature of the fight. You are battling both the surface waves coming in and the undertow going out. But you can't see the undertow. It's the hidden flow of water below the surface that is moving in the opposite direction of the surface current.

Have you ever fought an undertow? Apparently, the Apostle Paul did. "I do not understand my own actions," he wrote to the early Christians in Rome, "For I do not do what I want, but I do the very thing I hate."[6] Most of us can relate. There are forces in the shadows of our subconscious that can undercut even our best intentions. A seasoned guide will help us understand why.

Certainly, in Jesus's story of the prodigal son, the younger son had some stuff going on under the surface. Something was driving him to ditch his home and family and set out on a grand journey of self-discovery. Ironically, in his all-out search for himself, he felt more lost than ever.

A while back, I met a twenty-something woman who had grown up in a small town and couldn't wait to leave it behind. She was destined for bright city lights, dreams come true, and total freedom to be herself. Surprisingly, after a couple of years in the big city, she moved back. No one was quite sure why. When I asked, she said, "It was fun . . . for a while. But I found myself doing more and more things that weren't me. At one point, I was so far away from myself, I didn't know who I was anymore. I felt lost. I had to come home."

The younger son had walked that road. Broke. Far from home. Famished. He, too, was feeling pretty lost. When he began to be in need, he suddenly came to himself and thought, "I don't have to starve in this God-forsaken place. My father's hired hands have plenty to eat. I could go home, apologize to my father, and work as a hired hand."[7] With this new plan he could make things right with his father *and* redeem himself in the eyes of others. It was brilliant! The whole idea compelled him to head home.

You may be thinking, "If this is where the younger son's story shifts, where is his guide? He's out in a field by himself feeding pigs. Was the farmer who employed him his guide? Did his father say something to him before he left home that finally rang true? If so, why didn't Jesus put that in the story?"

Perhaps Jesus didn't name a guide because he wanted to point to a guide who can meet us wherever we are. When Jesus is preparing to bodily leave this earth, he tells his disciples about someone his Heavenly Father will send in his name. Translators of the original language use various names to capture who this person is: Counselor, Advocate, Companion. Whatever the title, the person the Father sends is the Holy Spirit, the very Spirit of Jesus, who takes up residence in our lives at our request. Jesus says one of the key roles of the Holy Spirit is to "guide you in all truth."[8] Both in the Bible and in our lives, God sometimes uses human guides and sometimes provides direct guidance through the Holy Spirit, the Spirit of Truth.

Guides can help us come back from a fall by leading us through three tests of character: owning our mistakes before God and others, receiving forgiveness, and deciding to make the journey back.

Honest to God

As both the younger son and David found, one of the early steps on the long road back from a fall often involves an honest confession: "There are some things I've messed up. Some of them very badly. And they are my fault."

Confession is simply being honest with God about what you both know is true. God is all present and all knowing. God is not going to say, "Wow! I never knew that!" The challenge for all of us is to find the courage and humility to own up to the truth. You might say, "OK, God, I know you know this about me. Now, I am going to admit it to you. This is what I have said. This is what I have done. This is what I should have done but didn't. I am not proud of it. But that's how it went down."

Generally, a good confession includes three parts:

- Examine one's conscience
- Experience godly sorrow
- Expect to avoid sin[9]

I'm aware this topic may feel uncomfortable. Let me put you at ease. There is no one you know who has not had a fall of some kind. It is a part of the human condition. Scripture says, "All have sinned and fall short of the glory of God."[10] You, me, everyone. You are not alone. No one is being singled out. There is nothing new or surprising about selfish or prideful words, thoughts, or actions that hurt God, others, and ourselves.

But if we ever hope to get free of such things and start our comeback, we must come clean and share the exact nature of them with God. It doesn't do any good to say, "Oh Lord, forgive me for everything." A good confession begins by being specific. "Forgive me for doing or saying this thing to this person at this time."

As we examine our conscience, we should naturally experience sorrow. There may be tears and the like, but it doesn't have to be emotional. In fact, it's possible to simply feel bad because of what it cost us and never realize the pain it caused God.

A good confession involves godly sorrow—a keen awareness of the deep offense our pride or selfishness has been to God and a genuine regret for the hurt it has caused to all involved.

Finally, a good confession expects to avoid repeating the behavior in the future.

I once talked to a mom whose son kept doing things that hurt her and others. She kept excusing him. "He feels sorry afterward. I know he does. He says, 'I'm sorry, Mom. I'm really sorry.' But he keeps on doing the same thing."

I may have surprised her with my reply: "I don't mean to sound harsh, but he's not asking for forgiveness. He's asking for *permission*. He wants you to let him off the hook, so he can do it again. If he felt real sorrow over the pain he's causing, he would be sorry enough to quit—to stop the hurtful behavior."

A good confession expects a change in behavior. Given all that, here's part of David's confession after Nathan confronted him. It comes from the Old Testament of the Bible:

> Have mercy on me, O God,
> according to your unfailing love;
> according to your great compassion
> blot out my transgressions.
> Wash away all my iniquity
> and cleanse me from my sin.
>
> For I know my transgressions,
> and my sin is always before me.
> Against you, you only, have I sinned
> and done what is evil in your sight;
> so you are right in your verdict
> and justified when you judge. . . .
>
> My sacrifice, O God, is a broken spirit;
> a broken and contrite heart
> you, God, will not despise.
>
> Psalm 51:1-4, 17 (NIV)

David is totally honest with God. He shares the exact nature of his wrong, and you can hear in his words the deep sorrow he feels over it—a godly sorrow for the pain it caused God. And he never wants to do that again. David discovered a sobering truth: *without confession, there is no comeback.*

Once we have made our confession, we move on to the test of forgiveness.

Receive Total Forgiveness

In a former church, a woman called me one day and asked if we could talk. I could tell by her voice it was quite serious. She said, "I don't want to meet at the church because I'm afraid someone might overhear our conversation." I agreed to meet her in a neutral place that would protect her confidentiality.

As she began to speak, tears came to her eyes. "This is so hard to say." She told me, "I never wanted to have to tell anyone this. But something you said on Sunday made me realize that I had to tell someone." She paused.

"I had an affair. No one knows about it. It is a secret I have been carrying around for a long time. After a while, we realized how wrong it was, and we ended it. But the guilt I still feel has been eating me alive. I don't know how to tell my husband. I don't know if he will be able to forgive me. But I had to tell someone. I couldn't bear it anymore. Do you think God could forgive me?"

Freeze-frame it right there. What would you say? This was a woman with strong faith. She knew how deeply her actions had hurt God's heart and her own. She confessed her sin to God and to another person. What was she still seeking? To be free from the guilt she had carried for so long.

We talked about God's total forgiveness. The penalty for her sins and mine had been paid in full by Christ's death on the cross. He died for us, so we wouldn't have to be locked in a prison of our own wrongs.

She had already placed her faith in Jesus. Now came her test. Would she trust Christ's complete forgiveness in her life, or would she keep trying to pay for her sin by beating herself up with relentless guilt? Only she could decide.

With trembling faith, she prayed that day to receive the forgiveness Christ alone could offer. She later confessed to her husband, and he forgave her too. To this day, she is a loving wife and mother, a vital member of her church, and a radiant woman of faith.

When David confessed, he received an assurance of God's forgiveness through Nathan:

> Nathan replied, "The LORD has taken away your sin. You are not going to die."
>
> 2 Samuel 12:13 (NIV)

Although David had knowingly done terrible things and didn't deserve to be forgiven, God showed him grace—an unconditional love that claimed him as he was, forgave his sins, and lifted him to a new life. God's grace did not stop the painful consequences of his actions from playing out, both in his family and his kingdom, but it did restore David's close relationship with God and redeem his life for a completely different second half.

That leaves the final test.

Decide to Come Back

When the TCU football team went into the locker room at halftime down 31–0, they had a decision to make. Are we just going to roll over, or are we going to come back?

After a bad first half, you can see what David decided as he prayed from the heart:

> Restore to me the joy of your salvation
> and grant me a willing spirit, to sustain me.
> Then I will teach transgressors your ways,
> so that sinners will turn back to you.
>
> Psalm 51:12-13 (NIV)

David knew if God would restore him, God would use him again. Not because he was a model of right living, but because he was a trophy of God's grace.

You may think what you have done has disqualified you from God's service. "God can't use me. I blew it. I'm damaged goods." But that's not what God thinks about you.

God loves comebacks. Look at David. In one fell swoop, he broke seven of the ten commandments. He put Bathsheba before God and made her an idol. He killed, committed adultery, stole Uriah's wife, lied, and coveted someone who did not belong to him.

By all rights, he should be a mere footnote in the history of God's people. Yet we remember him today as the shepherd boy who became Israel's greatest king, a man after God's own heart, and the author of the twenty-third psalm as well as more than seventy other psalms in the Bible. It was David's throne that God chose to establish forever, and it was his royal bloodline that one day led to the birth of Jesus. Even still, confronting his grievous wrongs was the biggest giant he ever faced.

After his epic fall, David could have rolled over and given up—his reputation in ruins. But he didn't. He decided to come back. And God still uses his life and his words to inspire people throughout the world nearly three thousand years after his death.

What's the larger lesson here? Don't give up. Don't do it. God has more in store for your life than you know right now. There are things being worked out that you can't see, but if you give up now, you will short-circuit the plan. Give it time. Let it come. The most meaningless statistic in football is the halftime score.

Do you know why God loves comebacks? Because every person God has ever used is a comeback story from their own unique falls. That's all God has to work with.

Maybe you've had an epic fall somewhere along the line. Maybe no one even knows about it right now except you—you and God.

Here's some good news: you don't have to stay locked in a prison of past mistakes. Seek wise counsel. Find a guide who will help you get honest with God and others, receive total forgiveness, and decide to come back!

When by God's grace you do, it will set you up to make a comeback plan and get cracking.

Chapter 4

Hope-Filled Action

Without goals, and plans to reach them,
you are like a ship that has set sail with no destination.

—Fitzhugh Dodson

The scene is etched in my mind. After leaving at 3:00 a.m. to catch a plane to the Caribbean, fifteen travel-weary souls crammed into the back of a ramshackle truck as the sun began to set. Sitting shoulder-to-shoulder, we shared a sweaty ride for ninety minutes in ninety-degree heat. By the time we reached our remote destination, night had fallen. With no electricity in that part of the island, we scouted out our sleeping quarters by flashlight.

As I came around the outside of the bunk house, my light fell on a Haitian man having an animated cell phone conversation in Creole. I soon discovered he would serve as our guide, translator, and gracious host. Bleary-eyed by then, I couldn't quite make out the white letters printed on his grey t-shirt. As I drew closer, I saw there were just three words: "I am hope." Only later did I discover their true meaning.

It was March 2013, and the mission team from our church had arrived to work with other Midwest mission teams to build "Homes for Haitians" in the wake of the 7.0 magnitude earthquake that decimated Haiti in 2010.

Although three years had passed, the devastation was still fresh as we traveled in and around the capital city of Port-au-Prince. Even now I can't wrap my mind around the catastrophic level of suffering. Due to the severity of the quake, its aftershocks, and a lack of building codes, the death toll was somewhere between 220,000 and 300,000 people. Another 300,000 people were injured, and 1.5 million people were initially displaced.[1]

Estimates of those affected by the quake include some three million people—nearly one-third of the country's total population.[2] And each of them had a story.

As our mission trip unfolded, our guide shared his. Jean Claude Degazan was born and raised in Haiti, in a family of humble means. He was grateful to receive a good education, and as an adult he became a translator for church mission teams.

On January 12, 2010, he was working in a place called Petit-Goâve with a medical team. They were inside a makeshift clinic performing eye surgeries free of charge. Suddenly, the ground shook. He looked up at the concrete ceiling, and it began to sink a foot or two at a time in rapid succession. Jean Claude took a step to try to escapte, but the building quickly collapsed. Buried by all kinds of concrete debris, incredibly, he did not lose consciousness.

Imagine what that must have been like. Pinned under jagged slabs of concrete. Unable to move. Yet somehow you are still alive and conscious. How would you react? What's the first thing you'd do? The decision came easy for Jean Claude.

> I talked to God. I said, "God, are you going to leave me where I'm at?" And I heard a voice saying that you can do something. I didn't know what I could do because of everything on top of me. There were bricks and rebar. It was very difficult for me.
>
> And for the second time I said, "God, there is nothing I can do." And the voice kept saying, "You can do something." Finally, I tried to move my arms, and I couldn't. Move my legs. I couldn't.
>
> For the third time I said to God, "There is no way for me to do it." And the voice kept saying, "You can do something." And I said, "If God said so, then I am going to do something."
>
> And I pulled my arm out, my right arm. It's typical for me to have my cell phone in my hand texting people. When my arm got out with my cell phone in my hand, I texted one of my nephews that was there. He immediately shouted to my friend, another interpreter who got out of the building, "Jean Claude is alive!" They all thought I had died. My friend said, "Jean Claude is alive! I'm going to save him!"
>
> I heard them saying that, but I couldn't call out to them. Instead, I pulled my hand back again as the Holy Spirit led me. I put my cell phone on my leg, and I took some of the rock off the top of my head without knowing what I was doing at the time. Finally, my head cleared off and I could see outside. Then I cried for help. I called to my friend, "I am here! Could you help me?"

His friend and his nephew quickly found Jean Claude, removed the concrete tomb encasing him, and pulled him to safety without a single broken bone! They also pulled four other people from the rubble alive. A sixth person pinned in the same building died.

Of course, Jean Claude was now worried sick about his wife and kids. At that point there was no way to communicate with his family. No cell service to that part of the island. No transportation. Nothing. Shaken but determined, he set out on foot. When he reached his house, he found it had collapsed. Refusing to look through the ruins, he asked his neighbors if they had seen his family. They told him his wife had gone to a safe place after the quake. Racing to that shelter, he soon found her. They fell into each others arms and shed tears of joy. His wife then explained how she had just left home to buy something to cook for the kids when the quake hit, and thank God, their kids were still in school. Everyone was alive and safe!

When Jean Claude paused for a moment, no one knew what to say. We sat spellbound as he painted this heroic story on the dark backdrop of such devastating loss. Frankly, it was hard to take it all in. Hollywood couldn't write a script like this. No one would believe it.

Just as we thought this comeback story had come to a close, Jean Claude described how it changed his life. He knew hundreds of thousands of people lost their lives or lost family members, and he could easily have been one of them. Naturally, a person wonders, "Why me?" "Why did I survive?" His only explanation was this: "I realized that if I am alive, that should be for a reason."

Jean Claude's stunning story is a master's course on the inner workings of a comeback. As always, it started with a fall. In this case the fall was a natural disaster completely beyond Jean Claude's control. Many times it's a poor decision or an inappropriate behavior we now regret. In each case, it brings us face-to-face with a choice. Will that fall define and defeat us, or will it motivate us toward a turnaround?

After a fall, our most natural response is to wallow in self-pity. Given his traumatic situation, Jean Claude felt trapped not just outwardly but inwardly. Although God whispered that Jean Claude could do something, he dismissed the idea completely, twice. He knew he was stuck. Why couldn't God see that too?

After a fall, it's easy to get stuck in a place of perceived helplessness. Sadly, some never make it out. But for most there comes a point, perhaps when we are about to lose something we're not prepared to live without, when we come to our senses. We realize that, regardless of what happened, it's time to take responsibility for our own issues, climb back on the horse, and start riding again. This deep, inner decision sets us on a new course.

In most cases, the road back is long, with blind turns and hairpin curves, none of which are well-marked. We can go it alone, but our chances of getting lost or sidetracked by alluring detours are high. Our best bet is to find a trustworthy guide who can help us navigate this unpredictable journey. Jean Claude immediately turned to prayer. Even though it didn't make sense at the time, Jean Claude chose to trust God's whisper instead of his deep sense of helplessness. That single choice saved his life as well as the lives of several people around him.

Ironically, Jean Claude had two advantages in this horrific situation. First, he knew he must do something or he would die. It was both urgent and important to take action. In most cases, the issues before us are not that clear. Second, he knew an earthquake was not his fault. He didn't have to wade through the guilt of being responsible for his own fall. Both of these factors freed him to respond more quickly and decisively.

A lack of motivation and emotional baggage are two roadblocks that bring many comeback journeys to a dead stop. Often our regret leads to a paralysis of analysis that sounds like this: "It's all my fault. If I had not said those things or behaved in that way, none of this would have happened. I always do something like this. Why even try to turn things around? It never works."

Sound familiar? A silo of self-pity is a dark place to live. Thankfully, we don't have to set up shop there. Every time someone says, "Why even try?" there are two issues going on below the surface. At one level, there's a secret hope that this time will be different. Deep down, each of us yearns for dreams to be fulfilled, relationships to be mended, and turnarounds to succeed.

Yet, on another level, there's an overwhelming sense of being stuck. Comeback attempts have fallen short just enough times to make us believe trying again is useless. In these situations, we succumb to what Michael Hyatt calls the "Cynicism Spiral."

The spiral begins when your hopes for a comeback are disappointed. Ongoing disappointment leads to frustration, which is followed quickly by anger. Prolonged anger turns into sadness and ultimately depression—a form of anger turned inward. The spiral culminates with cynicism—a self-protective behavior we all use to insulate us from more disappointment.[3]

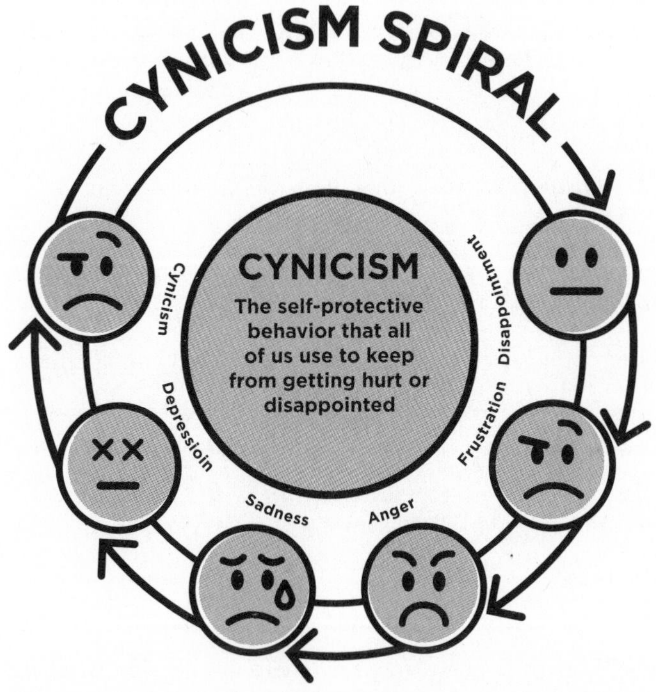

When you have had a fall and tried to come back previously, you might have experienced one or more of these emotions. I certainly have. It's a natural reaction. Thankfully, there is a process that can move us beyond cynicism and return us to the comeback journey.

But first, be aware of the danger. If we hold on to cynicism, it will sabotage the results of this process. Cynicism may be the single greatest factor keeping us stuck right where we are. We begin to move forward only when we listen to our emotions without being controlled by them. As author Peter Scazzero notes, "You cannot change what you are unaware of."[4]

Overcoming the Cynicism Spiral involves a four-part process that we are already halfway through:

1. **Conviction.** Realize something needs to change.

2. **Compelled.** Discover your inspiration to move forward.

3. **Course.** Chart the specific steps necessary.

4. **Action.** Start with small wins to build momentum.

Transforming Practice: Plan and Act

The comeback practices at this stage are chart a course and take action, but they are built on the foundations of conviction and a sense of being compelled found in the two previous chapters. Let's put all four together, starting with conviction.

Conviction

In Jesus's story of the prodigal son, it took a while for the younger son to play his hand all the way out. He snatched his share of his father's inheritance, set off for a far country, and carelessly wasted it on his every desire. Flat broke and unwilling to admit defeat, he hired himself out to a farmer who sent him out to a field to feed pigs.

Until this point, the younger son had marched through life with a self-absorbed certainty any dictator would applaud. But even he couldn't reconcile his self-image with his circumstances. As he stood in that field, hungry and alone, he suddenly saw his life for the charade he had made it. In Jesus's words, "He came to himself."[5]

This is the necessary first step to stopping the egoistic madness. For the first time in his life, the younger son experienced a sense of conviction. He realized something was not right, something deep within him. It was painful, to be sure, but it became a saving grace.

Psychologist and author Henry Cloud describes it this way, "We change our behavior when the pain of staying the same becomes greater than the pain of changing. Consequences give us the pain that motivates us to change."[6]

Understanding just how far he had fallen, the younger son now begins the next part of the process.

Compelled

When the pain of staying the same finally got his attention, the younger son was motivated to reexamine his life. For the first time, it dawned on him that his father's hired hands were treated really well, far better than his experience in this distant place. Growing up, he never thought twice about the way the hired men were treated. Didn't everyone give their employees more food than they could eat? Maybe there were some things he took for granted about his father, things he didn't appreciate until he left home. That's when it clicked. "I don't have to live like this. I can go home, apologize to my father, and redeem myself."

This new idea brought a burst of new energy. For the first time in a long time, he felt hope. Of course, he could not return as a son. He had burned that bridge. But the thought of going back to a place he knew, where he would have plenty of food, and where he could have a chance to start over, ignited a new dream in his heart. It compelled him to start the journey home.

When we have a fall, it's not enough to simply come to a point of conviction. That gets us motivated to break out of our rut, but it doesn't call us forward. It's the push without a pull.

Make no mistake, it's crucial to conclude that we can't stay "here" any longer. Staying the same is not an option. We must move on.

But we also need a picture of a preferable future. What will this new life look like, smell like, and feel like? How will we know when we have arrived? And most importantly, why is going there worth the effort?

To motivate ourselves or anyone else to step into a new future, we must start with "Why."[7] It's what great leaders in every arena do that the rest of us miss.

Author Simon Sinek looks at it from a business perspective:

> Very few people or companies can clearly articulate WHY they do WHAT they do. When I say WHY, I don't mean to make money—that's a result. By WHY I mean what is your purpose, cause or belief? WHY does your company exist? WHY do you get out of bed every morning? And WHY should anyone care?[8]

He contends that most people start with *what* they do (for example, build computers) and then tell you *how* they do it (with the latest technology and attractive design), but very few can tell you *why* they do these things. He calls this an outside-in approach based on his "Golden Circle."

Instead of moving from the outside in, the world's most inspiring leaders and organizations think, act, and communicate in the opposite way. They move from the inside out. They start with *why.*

Sinek summarizes Apple's communication style as an example:

> Everything we do, we believe is challenging the status quo. We believe in thinking differently.
>
> The way we challenge the status quo is by making our products beautifully designed, simple to use and user-friendly.
>
> And we happen to make great computers.
>
> Wanna buy one?

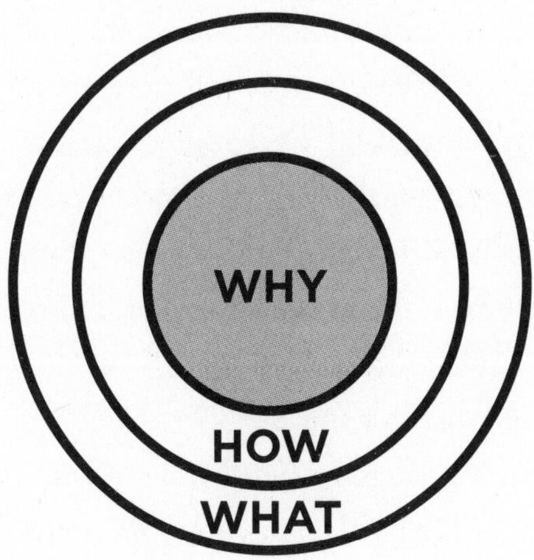

Why. How. What. Apple's reason to buy is not based on *what* they do, but *why* they do it.[9]

Why do you do *what* you do? Can you state clearly *why* you get out of bed and head off to school or go to work? (Remember, it's not to make money. That's a result.) Why do you take care of your family, attend worship, serve in the community, spend time with friends, or start a new project? Is there a deeper purpose? Without a strong *why*, your level of engagement will surely wane. You will find yourself focusing on *what* you have to do (I have to do this today and then I have to do that) and forget your *why* altogether. *What* without *why* leads to an endless stream of tasks disconnected from any larger picture. Too many people know how this plays out. You soon lose interest, start going through the motions, and trudge through life emotionally flatlined. Gail Hyatt says it well, "People lose their way when they lose their why."[10]

I can relate. After years of juggling many responsibilities in an overcrowded schedule, I knew I needed a deep slow down. I drove to a retreat center in another state and took an eight-day silent prayer retreat. Here's what that meant for me.

For eight days, I went off TV, social media, and the internet (with one brief exception). Over the course of that time, I had three one-hour talks with my spiritual director, Father Bill Creed, whom I introduced in the previous chapter. I also talked briefly with my wife, Leanne, most nights. But the vast majority of that time, I spent alone and in silence.

I was on retreat because I needed to hear from God in a way my normal pace of life would not allow. To intensify my prayer time, I fasted from food for the first three days. I wanted God to have my full attention.

By the end of the second day, it became apparent that somewhere along the line, I had lost my *why*. It had gotten muddled in a myriad of tasks and concerns. Slowly, unknowingly, I had made my life about so many other things than who I was at my core.

While reading through some of my old journals, I ran across a quote I had heard in a sermon years ago that I had forgotten. It was from Maya Angelou. She said, "To really love someone is to know the song their heart sings and to hum it back to them on the days they forget."[11]

That night, just before going to bed, I wrote in my journal:

God, hum it back to me. I've forgotten.

The next morning, shortly after waking up, five words popped in my head, "Because people matter to me."

I blurted out, "That's it! It's so simple! It's the core of the gospel. For God so loved the world, he gave his only Son. It's proof of God's extraordinary love for us."

In that moment, I remembered what was already in me. The song of my heart is to help people discover they matter to God. That's what my life is about.

It is difficult to describe the rush of energy released within me when I reconnected with my *why*. It compelled me to reengage with my core mission on a whole new level.

Course

When we come to the conviction that something needs to change and we discover a compelling vision of a preferable future, the next step is to chart a course to get there.

When the prodigal son realized he needed to go back to his father, he immediately put together a strategy. It started with an apology.

> "Father, I have sinned against heaven and against you.
> I no longer deserve to be called your son.
> Take me on as one of your hired hands."
>
> Luke 15:18-19 (CEB)

Once he had that speech down, he headed for home.

Regardless of the kind of comeback you need, charting a course of action is crucial to any true turnaround. Whether you want to go back for your degree, repair a relationship, relaunch a business, recover from an addiction, or lose weight, there is no success without a strategy. You have to think through what it will require of you. Jesus said,

> But don't begin until you count the cost. For who would begin construction of a building without first calculating the cost to see if there is enough money to finish it? Otherwise, you might complete only the foundation before running out of money, and then

> everyone would laugh at you. They would say, "There's the person who started that building and couldn't afford to finish it!"
>
> Luke 14:28-30 (NLT)

Sometime back, I saw a church begin a massive new expansion just off a busy interstate. Large steel beams were put in place to form the outline of an addition that would more than double their space. You could feel the optimism of the congregation as you drove by. Since I only travel that highway occasionally, I didn't think about the project after that. Five years later I happened to pass that church again, and nothing had changed. A sinking feeling came over me. Something went seriously wrong. It's now been over twenty years, and those same steel beams stand framing the air.

Counting the cost is just as crucial in a comeback. Author and pastor Nelson Searcy lists the multiple advantages of carefully charting a course to get from where you are to where you want to be. A strategy . . .

- provides structure for the journey,
- forces you to think on paper,
- provides focus,
- drives research,
- saves time, and
- makes it easier to ask others for help

Each one is a boon for a comeback bid, but the time advantage alone is worth the exercise. Searcy notes, "For every minute you spend planning, you save an hour in implementation."[12]

Abraham Lincoln said it this way, "If you give me six hours to cut down a tree, I will spend the first four hours sharpening the axe."

Charting a course involves two parts: setting goals and breaking them down into bite-sized tasks. For goal-setting, I've found the SMART acronym a helpful tool.

- **Specific:** Nothing becomes dynamic until it becomes specific. Vague goals don't inspire us.
- **Measurable:** The desired result must be defined in quantifiable terms.
- **Achievable:** The goal stretches a person without being unrealistic and includes necessary resources.
- **Relevant:** The goal aligns with values, season of life, and other goals.
- **Time-Bound:** Each goal is assigned a completion date.

Once your SMART goals are set, you discern the tasks necessary to accomplish them and schedule those tasks into your calendar. Chances are the whirlwind of your everyday life will not suddenly die down and leave behind large chunks of free time. To make any real progress toward a comeback, you must intentionally set aside time in your calendar. What gets scheduled, gets done.

Here's what that might look like. Let's say you have a one-year goal. You could break it down into quarterly segments. What needs to be done in the next three months? That quarterly goal could be broken down into one-month targets. Follow that with one-week tasks. You then block out time in your schedule to do these smaller pieces. You might realize, "Well, to get started on this goal, I need to go out to lunch with this person who has had great success in this area and ask about best practices. I'm good at lunch. How about Tuesday?"

Make appointments the way you would if someone called and asked to meet with you. In essence, you are meeting with your goal. Your goals are the grand scale of what you want to accomplish. Scheduling tasks is the granular scale. There's nothing grand without a granular plan.

Action

Charting a good course sets you up for the fun part—taking action! The best-laid plans are useless until you jump into the fray. In the action phase, our biggest challenges are to stay granular and stay the course. We love a splashy goal that snags attention. We're going to reinvent the company to once again be a leader in its industry or renovate the entire house to bring it back to its former glory. Maybe we've decided to take back our health by losing fifty pounds. We announce it with fanfare and are filled with optimism. Nothing feels better than the first four hours of a diet.

Sadly, we often set big goals and get small results.[13] That demoralizes us, and we give up. Organizational theorist Karl Weick noticed this same pattern when addressing large social problems such as hunger or crime.

In his now-famous article on redefining the scale of social problems, he writes, "People often define social problems in ways that overwhelm their ability to do anything about them."[14] Many people feel the same way about their lofty comeback goals. They deeply desire to see them accomplished but don't know where to start. This makes planning at a granular level all but impossible.

Weick's solution is to shift our focus from the overwhelming goal to a small win. He defines a small win as "a concrete, complete, implemented outcome of moderate importance."[15]

By itself, one small win may not seem like much. But it makes a second win easier. And then a third. As one small solution falls into place, it reveals the next solvable problem. People and resources start to flow to the wins. Old opponents begin to change their behavior.[16] In ways that were previously unimaginable, real hope for reaching a large goal is born.

I confess, when I first ran across this concept, I was far more enamored with the flashy win. "I'm a big-picture guy," I would say. It was my excuse not to be bothered with the small stuff. Yet I knew all too well that overwhelming feeling of "where do I start?" In an attempt to get traction on a larger goal of administrative effectiveness, I decided to pick a small win and see what would happen.

It was a simple thing, really: clear off my desk at home. Over months, I had stacked so many mounds of paper, there was little room to work. One night, I spent three hours going through the piles, pitching and sorting. When I finished, I found a desk! It was invigorating. Completing this concrete, little task gave me energy to tackle the next task with fresh confidence.

It's counterintuitive, but to get really BIG things done, you start with small wins—like cleaning off your desk—and build momentum. Visible progress propels you toward the next win and the next one, until you make a real breakthrough.

Every comeback is a journey. Each of these four parts—conviction, compelled, course, and action—is indispensable to a turnaround. As a group, they build on one another and reinforce one another. If one is left out, a major comeback is unlikely, but together these four elements create a formidable force for new life.

The kids in Cabaret, Haiti, can attest to this. Remember Jean Claude's conviction after he was rescued. "I realized that if I am alive, that should be for a reason."

Shortly after the earthquake, he was working with a mission team at the Methodist church in Cabaret, a small town in a rural area called Arcahaie about ninety minutes north of Port-au-Prince. On his way there, he saw lots of kids who were not in school. When he asked around, he was told the parents couldn't afford private education and the government of Haiti did not provide public schools.

Immediately, he knew something had to change. "This is not fair," he told others. Jean Claude's education was made possible because several people outside Haiti invested in him. As he reflected on the dilemma, he asked God, "How can I pay that back to someone else?"

As he kept praying about this day after day, he saw only one picture in his mind: the children. The combination of their hope-filled eyes and a future without education broke his heart. He couldn't bear to leave these kids in the cruel grip of poverty, so he came up with a plan.

Each time he worked with mission teams as a translator, he would save some of the money they paid him. Of course, he gave most of his salary to his wife to take care of their family, but after each job, he put something back for the community in Arcahaie. Once he reached a certain amount, he met with the mayor and said, "I would like to have a piece of land, so I could build a school for the kids who don't go to school." The mayor was pleased to sell him some land and thanked him for his heart for people. Jean Claude said, "Well, if I am alive that should be for a reason. I don't know the reason, but that should be for a reason."

As soon as the land was in hand, he built a makeshift shelter for the school, mostly out of discarded building materials. It wasn't pretty, but it was a beginning. At that point, Jean Claude realized, "I need someone else to help me do it." Through a number of mission trips, Jean Claude had become friends with Dave and Cindy, who you met in Chapter 2. With passion in his voice, he told them the story of the earthquake, his rescue, and the conviction he felt about the children of Arcahaie. He said, "I have a problem here. We have a lot of kids who don't go to school and want to go to school. Here's my vision: to build a school for them. Here's what I've been doing. Could you help me?"[17]

Jean Claude's heartfelt appeal rocked Dave and Cindy to the core. They agreed to go back to their church and friends in the US and ask for their support. With joy, their congregation agreed to offer significant resources to unleash compassion for children and their families in Arcahaie. By sheer grace, the School of Hope was born in 2012.

Since then, Dave and Cindy have made twelve trips to Haiti—with more on the horizon. Now retired, their latest project is to build a guesthouse next to the school to host mission teams, serve as a community center, and be used as a marketplace for local goods and produce. With Haiti's unemployment rate above 90 percent, a local market will help the financial well-being of the community as well as the sustainability of the school.

Today four hundred students attend kindergarten through eighth grade at the School of Hope. Nineteen teachers, staff, and workers lead the classes and oversee the children. The school operates through donations and mission teams who serve on site. Each day around noon the children receive a hot meal of beans and rice. For many it will be their only meal of the day.[18] The impact of the School of Hope on the community and the future of Haiti is beyond estimation. Amazingly, it all goes back to one man who saw something was not right, felt compelled to do something about it, charted a course, and took action. In his words, "If I am alive, that should be for a reason." Now he is hope to a new generation.

Chapter 5
Trust the Process

First there is the fall, and then we recover from the fall. Both are the mercy of God!

—Lady Julian of Norwich

She could light up any room. Her quick smile, joyful spirit, and humble heart drew people to her like a magnet. It made her a natural fit for our church's connection team that welcomes first-time guests each weekend. People just felt at ease around her. She was real.

One Sunday when she was still a relative newcomer, she stood before a thousand people and introduced herself in a way that caught people off guard.

"Hello, my name is Amy. I am an alcoholic, a drug addict, a mother, a liar, a cheater, a manipulator, a fiancée, a con artist, and a convicted felon. But most of all, I'm a child of God. I have spent the better half of my adult life trying to stray as far away as possible from God, religion, and spirituality. I didn't have a need for it. It just wasn't there. You all were perfect, and I was damaged goods. I honestly didn't even know what the grace of God meant or why someone would need Jesus. Was I worthy of a love of this magnitude anyway?"

Many that day were shocked. The person she described was not the person they knew at all. Until then, few people in the congregation had heard her backstory.

Amy didn't grow up in a churchgoing family. She had no connection to God or Jesus. Her only exposure to Christianity was going to her grandma's small-town church on Christmas and Easter.

At age eight, her self-described "pretty normal life" was decimated by her parents' divorce. Her dad moved to Florida and mostly dropped out of the picture. Her mom later remarried, but Amy didn't get along with her new stepdad. He made the family go to church, a practice Amy couldn't stand as a teenager. She didn't like getting dressed up and sitting still for what seemed like forever. That's when she started forming opinions about religion. In her eyes, the people seemed snobby. They thought they were better than everyone else.

Unfortunately, it wasn't just the people at church. Amy describes a pivotal moment when everything changed. "One morning as I was getting ready for church and taking too long, my stepdad started yelling at my mom and called me a few unfavorable names. At that point I said, 'If this is the type of people Christians are, then I don't want to be a part of that.' I held on to that morning for years."

Her addictive behaviors began early. As she got older, she started hanging out with the wrong crowd, trying to fit in some way. Although she was smart in school without even trying, she didn't like being smart. Didn't think it was cool. Rebelling against the "smart kid" tag led her down a destructive path.

"I used pot, alcohol, and relationships as my addictions in high school and on through college. But none of that really affected me the way cocaine did. I think having an addictive behavior was in my genes to begin with, and I just ran with it. In hindsight, I was trying to fill a void. I didn't feel good about myself, and all of that just snowballed into full-blown addiction.

"I am not sure when it went from recreational to necessity, but there was no turning back. I went to rehab seven different times. The one thing that always bothered me in the twelve-step program was the word *God*. I did not believe in God, nor did I see that as a way to get clean and sober. I thought it was ridiculous that people fell into that way of thinking. I was sure I could handle it myself."

Stuck, lonely, and afraid, Amy was certain the one thing she didn't need was to trust in a power higher than her own.

Her story has a lot in common with the mountain climber whose foot slipped halfway up the peak. As he began to fall, he quickly grabbed a tree branch. There he hung halfway between heaven and earth, unable to climb up and unable to climb down.

> After a while, he looked down into the valley and called out, "Help! Is there anybody there who can help me?"
>
> He listened intently, but all he could hear was the sound of his own frightened voice echoing through the valley—"who can help me? . . . who can help me?"
>
> He then looked up toward the top of the mountain. "Help!" he cried, "Is there anybody up there?"
>
> From the mountain top a voice said, "I am here. Do not be afraid."
>
> "Who are you?" the climber asked.
>
> "I am the Lord," the voice replied.

> "Wonderful!" the climber exclaimed. "Listen, Lord, I'm in trouble. Can you help me?"
>
> "Of course I can help you," the voice answered. "Just do as I say."
>
> "I'll do anything you say," the climber replied. "Just help me."
>
> The voice said, "Let go."
>
> For a long while, the climber was silent. Then he called back, "Is there anybody *else* up there?"[1]

Maybe you know someone who feels like they're on a cliff hanging on for dear life. Maybe that person is you. The last thing anyone wants to do at that moment is "let go." It would mean giving up what little control we have left and trusting it will all be OK. Who does that?

One day when I was hanging on a cliff of my own, I called my spiritual director and said, "I know I need to take some steps to come back, but I don't know if I can go through with it. Can you help me?"

He asked what I thought was a strange question. "Roger, how trustworthy is God?"

"What do you mean?" I replied.

He said, "Trust happens when the person we are in relationship with is trustworthy. Maybe you should ask, 'How trustworthy are you, God?'"

"Remember Abraham, the father of the Jewish nation?" he continued. "God called him to go to a land he knew nothing of. He had no idea how it would turn out. He just trusted that God was doing something good. You see, the opposite of trust is fear. Maybe God is inviting you to trust."

Like anyone hanging on the side of a cliff, that didn't make sense to me. But I was desperate, so I spent some time trying to figure out what Abraham was all about in the first book of the Bible, Genesis.

Abram, as he was known before God changed his name, was the oldest son of Terah and could trace his family line all the way back to Noah and the flood. Abram married Sarah, but she was unable to have children.

One day Terah loaded up his family, including his son Abram and Abram's wife, Sarah, and headed off to Haran. They left from Ur in what is now southern Iraq and traveled northwest along the Euphrates River to Haran. The family stayed in this flourishing caravan city for years until Terah died at a very old age. At that point, Abram remembered what the Lord had said to him back in Ur:

> Go from your country and your kindred and your father's house to the land that I will show you. I will make of you a great nation, and I will bless you, and make your name great, so that you will be a blessing. I will bless those who bless you, and the one who curses you I will curse; and in you all the families of the earth shall be blessed.
>
> Genesis 12:1-3 (NRSV)

Abram now faced a decision. If he chose to follow God's command, there would be no trip back home to Ur. Instead, he would be plunged into a process that would forever change him. When you have slipped off the-way-it-used-to-be mountain and are hanging on for dear life, God makes three invitations:

- Let go of the past in trust
- Let be an unseen future in hope
- Let grow God's work by love

I first heard this process described years ago by Francis Dorff in his book *The Art of Passingover*. Dorff's focus was on navigating life's transitions, which are merely comebacks in disguise. It all starts with letting go.

Let Go in Trust

God makes a steep ask right out of the gate. "Go." Abram was to abandon the land, his extended family, and his immediate family. One Bible scholar said, "God knows the difficulties of these three separations. Abram is to leave everything behind and trust himself to God's guidance. The goal is the land, and all Abram knows about the land is that God will show it to him."[2]

That leaves you kind of wanting, doesn't it? I can imagine Abram having a few questions. "So, Lord, what does this land look like? Who lives there? Is there something you want me to do? A little info would be nice, God."

We are not accustomed to this kind of journey. My parents went on an Alaskan cruise a few years ago. It was a longtime dream come true. Months before they left, they received full-color brochures with pictures of the places they would visit, the cruise liner they would take, and their accommodations along the way. It even had an itinerary telling them how many days or hours they would spend in each place.

They knew how long it would take to get there and exactly how much it would cost. It was a package deal. What's more, thousands of people had taken this trip before them. The company had worked out a system.

This is not the kind of invitation God makes. Abram had no idea what this promised land would look like, how long it would take to get there, how much it would cost, or even why God wanted him to go in the first place. His brochure never came.

All he got was, "Go from your country and your kindred and your father's house to the land that I will show you." He doesn't even know how long God wants him to be there.

Would you go?

We'd probably say, "No, thanks." We like what we have. And even if we don't like it that much, it's familiar to us. Comfortable. "Why should I risk what I have for something that is totally unknown to me?" someone might say.

No reason, really, until your life gets flipped. When cancer strikes, a child dies, a spouse walks out, or by some other means you're summoned to abandon your old life for a new one—suddenly, you no longer have what you had. You've slipped off the-way-it-used-to-be mountain. Now you're clinging for dear life to what you had as your feet dangle in the wind. The whiter your knuckles, the more stuck you become. As counter-intuitive as it may feel, the only way forward is to let go.

Letting go is exceedingly hard for human creatures because it means a painful ending. In essence, we feel like we are dying. Since we don't know what the future will look like, we fear it and hold on tightly to a life that no longer exists.

The prodigal son was a textbook example. When his inheritance money ran out and a famine hit the land, he doubled down and hung on tighter to his life in a far country. But as he fed pigs while his stomach growled, he suddenly saw in living color the shipwreck of his life. By the Spirit's guidance, he realized he didn't need to stay there, so he put together a plan to go home. To make the trip, he had to let go of his past in two ways. He first had to let his dream of being a big shot in a distant place go. He then had to let go of his place in his family. Sadly, his own actions had slammed those doors tight.

Once we let go of our past in trust, we enter phase two of this trust process.

Let Be in Hope

If you have ever watched a circus act, you may have marveled at a trapeze artist. High atop the circus tent, she swings from one bar to the next with the greatest of ease. But if you watch closely, there is an instant when the artist lets go of the first bar while waiting for the next bar to come in range. For one brief moment, she is suspended in midair. She's no longer holding the old bar but hasn't taken hold of the new one.

That is what it is like to "let be" an unseen future in hope. God didn't just say to Abram, "I want you to leave everything you know." God also said, "I want you to go to a land I will show you."

It's an awkward in-between. We aren't where we used to be, and we aren't where we are going. We are waiting, suspended in midair. On the comeback journey from a fall to our future, it's the toughest spot to be. The initial burst of excitement is gone, and the ultimate goal is still a distant glimmer. I call it the messy middle, and it stops many comebacks cold. It almost stopped golf's greatest star.

"I'm done," Tiger Woods told former pro Nick Faldo at the Masters Champions Dinner in 2017. After four knee operations and three back surgeries, Woods was more concerned about living a normal life than playing tour golf. "I could barely walk. I couldn't sit. Couldn't lay down. I really couldn't do much of anything," he recounted. But spinal fusion surgery on April 19, 2017, changed his life and his golf game.[3]

Make no mistake, it was a long road back. Woods's epic fall in 2009 was followed by a couple of lackluster years on tour. He bounced back with two stellar seasons, including five wins and the top of the money list in 2013. After that, back and knee injuries caught up with him. He missed all of 2016 and played only once in 2017.[4] Following his fourth back surgery, he slowly began to play his way into golf shape. At the end of 2018, he won his first tournament in five years. That set him up the following April for his favorite major of the year, the Masters.

Tiger started the final round of the 2019 Masters two strokes behind the leader. Although he had won fourteen major tournaments, he had never won without at least a share of the lead going into the final day. His first nine holes kept him in contention, and then came the fireworks on the back nine. The crowd's anticipation climbed to fever pitch. They could smell history in the making.

On the iconic par 5 fifteenth hole, Tiger sunk a birdie putt to take the lead for the first time in the tournament. The crowd came unhinged. At the Masters, there are roars and then there are Tiger roars. Tiger followed with a birdie on the sixteenth to deafening cheers. On the final hole, he tapped in his putt for a one-stroke victory and his fifth Masters title. It had been fourteen years since his last Masters win and eleven years since he had won a major. Tiger's victory at Augusta that day has been widely acclaimed as one of the greatest comebacks in sports history.

Yet two years before, he thought his career was over. Injuries, pain, and personal issues nearly tanked his comeback. He reluctantly considered throwing in the towel. Who could blame him?

Even in 2017, many considered him the greatest golfer of all time. It would have been easy, and many would say prudent, to quit. This is the undertow of the messy middle. It gets so hard to stay focused with such a long way to go. The daily-ness of the process messes with your mind. What was once clear turns fuzzy. Frankly, the easiest place to lose your way is in the middle.

I can attest. In the midst of a personal comeback, I realized some things in my soul had turned fuzzy. These were not the kind of issues that could be fixed in a single session with God—even a long one. I needed extended time to be still and listen.

My previous retreat changed my life, but three years had passed and I could feel it. With considerable effort, I carved out five days, showed up at a retreat center, and waited in silence. Not surprisingly, my time away started with a heartfelt desire for clarity. I needed to hear from God about some specific areas of my life. I wanted to know the precise steps I should take. Surely, the Lord would oblige. To my chagrin, the whole endeavor got derailed when I ran across this story from Brennan Manning's book *Ruthless Trust*:

> When the brilliant ethicist John Kavanaugh went to work for a month at "the house of the dying" in Calcutta, he was seeking a clear answer as to how best to spend the rest of his life. On the first morning there he met Mother Teresa. She asked, "And what can I do for you?" Kavanaugh asked her to pray for him.
>
> "What do you want me to pray for?" she asked. He voiced the request he had borne thousands of miles from the United States: "Pray that I have clarity."
>
> "No," Mother Teresa said firmly, "I will not do that."
>
> When he asked her why, she said, "Clarity is the last thing you are clinging to and must let go of."
>
> When Kavanaugh commented that she always seemed to have the clarity he longed for, she laughed and said, *"I have never had clarity; what I have always had is trust. So I will pray that you trust God."*[5]

To be honest, the thought that clarity was "the last thing you are clinging to and must let go of" kind of stung me. "What's so wrong with wanting clarity?" I inwardly protested. Only several days into the retreat was I able to see my push for clarity for what it really was—a desire for control. I keep learning that God doesn't invite us to control things. It's above our wisdom grade. Instead, we're invited to trust God for the many things we can't control. It's about surrender.

In the end, I didn't get the clarity I wanted on anything that week. All I got was a nudge to write about comebacks—because I needed one. And one other thing—a deeper trust in God.

When you're caught in the messy middle, it's not clarity that powers a comeback. It's *trust.* After three back surgeries, Tiger Woods trusted that a fourth one might actually work. He couldn't be sure. No one could guarantee it. But day by day, he trusted the long rehabilitation process, as well as the doctors, nutritionists, trainers, and coaches who created it. Back on tour, he learned once more how to trust himself under the high-stakes pressure of a major. Without a massive measure of trust, Tiger never would have stood on the eighteenth green as a Masters Champion for the fifth time.

Goals are good. Plans are important. But at some point on the comeback journey, you have to trust the process when you can't see the future. That's how the Bible defines faith:

> Faith is confidence in what we hope for and assurance about what we do not see.
>
> Hebrews 11:1 (NIV)

When the prodigal son set his sights on home, he had a precise plan in his head:

> I will get up and go to my father, and say to him,
> "Father, I have sinned against heaven and against you.
> I no longer deserve to be called your son.
> Take me on as one of your hired hands."
>
> Luke 15:18-19 (CEB)

With crystal clarity, he headed home, certain that his plan would save the day. But on his long journey back, he had plenty of time to think. Jesus doesn't mention this, but it's not hard to imagine less comforting thoughts crossing his mind.

> *What if my father refuses to speak to me?*
> *What if my father has died and my elder brother is in charge?*
> *My brother would never take me back, even as a hired hand.*
> *Is this really such a good plan?*

It's easy for doubts to creep in once the initial surge of optimism dies down. As he entered the messy middle, the younger son could have abandoned hope and headed back to the land of pig farms. Instead, he trusted the process, even though he couldn't know for sure how it would turn out.

This letting be an unseen future in hope does not mean we throw up our hands and say, "There's nothing we can do." It means we soberly stare into the future and say, *"There's nothing we can control."* We give ourselves too little and too much credit. Through personal effort, we can certainly increase our knowledge, but we can't make ourselves a genius. We can provide goods and services, but we can't make people buy them. We can treat people in loving ways, but we can't make someone love us—anymore than we can make a rose bloom. For creatures who crave control—creatures like us—this is a hard truth to own.

But once embraced, it liberates us from our self-appointed job of running the universe. We can lay down the fist-pounding heaviness of "make it happen" and instead live in the open-handed lightness of "let it come." We are still responsible for doing our part, but we stop imagining we control the outcome. We have influence, to be sure, but control is an illusion. This sober reality is what makes trust such a precious commodity.

How practical is the exercise of trust? Ask Tom Brady. With eight minutes left in the third quarter of the 2017 Super Bowl, his New England Patriots were down 28–3 to the Atlanta Falcons. For all intents and purposes, the game was over. Even the announcers had written them off. As the camera panned a dejected bench, Brady was caught moving up and down the sidelines preaching a different message. What could he possibly say to a team that had a 0.2 percent chance of winning? Three words. "Trust the process."

It was crazy to even entertain the idea. No team had ever won a Super Bowl when trailing by more than ten points. Brady knew that. He said post game, "Down 25 points, I mean, it's hard to imagine us winning." But they did imagine it. Against unthinkable odds, his teammates trusted him, and they trusted the process the coaches put together.[6]

Those three words ignited the greatest comeback in Super Bowl history. When the Patriots defeated the Falcons 34–28 in overtime, thirty-one NFL records were broken.[7]

Note how Brady and the Patriots handled their responsibility on the road back. He reportedly told his teammates, "Just do your jobs." And they did, at a very high level. But even when playing lights out, they easily could have run out of time, made a costly mistake, or been outplayed by their opponent at a crucial moment. It happens all the time. No matter how well or how hard they played, their effort alone could not guarantee a win. A whole host of things had to go their way that they could not control. Perhaps that's why no team had ever come back from such a deficit in the previous fifty Super Bowls. What the Patriots *could* do was offer their best and trust the process. The rest was out of their hands.

In the game of life, no one plays all four quarters well. Leads that seem insurmountable are sometimes squandered in minutes, and poor starts can be redeemed with just one second left on the clock. No matter how well we may have played, we all reach a point when it feels like life has run up the score and time is running out. If you are there now, don't worry about the future. Just focus on the next play and trust the process. God will take care of the final score.

Letting be our future in hope leads us to the culminating phase of the trust process.

Let Grow by Love

For our friend Abram, all this letting go and letting be didn't happen in a vacuum. It came with a super-charged promise that made no sense:

> I will make of you a great nation, and I will bless you, and make your name great, so that you will be a blessing . . . and in you all the families of the earth shall be blessed.
>
> Genesis 12:2-3 (NRSV)

At the time, Abram was seventy-five years old with no kids and a wife who was barren. The very idea was so ridiculous to his wife, Sarah, she laughed out loud. How exactly was God going to make of him a great nation? Humanly speaking, it was impossible.

There was only one hope. It involved a deep decision. Abram and Sarah had to trust the promise when they didn't understand it.

Not long ago, my wife and I faced a deep decision of our own. I was offered a wonderful job opportunity, but it would require us to leave the area where we had lived virtually our whole lives and move to a different state. I had some sense this was what I was supposed to do, but to be honest, I wasn't sure.

My wife and I prayed about it many times as we went back and forth in late-night wrestling matches with God. Finally, we had to fish or cut bait. After praying together one more time with no clear resolution, I said, "What do you think?"

She said, "Honey, I know it doesn't make any sense. We'll have to leave where we've lived most of our lives. We'll be three hours farther away from our aging parents and three hours farther from our two college-aged kids." She paused to hold back tears. "I'll have to give up a job I love, and you'll have to give up a job you love too. But I really believe this is who God made you to be."

Through her tender words, I heard the double ring of God's voice within hers. It's what I had been waiting for. "You're right," I said. "Let's do it." In that moment, trust broke through, and it led us on a completely new adventure to an unknown land.

You will never understand some promises until you trust them. After God's crazy promise to Abram, he took the risk of his life:

> So Abram went, as the LORD had told him.
>
> Genesis 12:4a (NRSV)

He trusted in God's promise, even though he didn't see how it could ever come true. Frankly, Abram faced a lot of dings and detours along the way. After arriving in what is modern-day Israel, Abram went through a deadly famine, a long trip to Egypt, lying about his marriage to save his skin, a great increase in riches, a bloody battle to save his nephew, and a son born to Sarah's maidservant to create a family line through human effort. None of these behaviors or experiences brought the promise one inch closer to fulfillment. Some of them appeared to push the pledged outcome further away. Twenty-four years after God first called him to a new land and promised to make him a great nation, Abram and Sarah still had no children. Imagine the heartbreak, the doubt. Most people would have given up long before, embittered by a God who didn't come through. But that's not Abram's story. Instead of destroying his faith, somehow Abram let the setbacks and disappointments of life deepen it.

You may be going through a messy middle of your own right now. You are not where you used to be, and you are not where you are going. You are somewhere in between a fall and your future. Worse yet, things keep happening that derail your progress—hard things like an accident or a betrayal, an illness or a sudden loss. Perhaps larger forces of unemployment, racism, or a natural disaster have thrown you into survival mode. Each time another wave hits, the comeback you dream of drifts further away. You don't want this. You don't even understand it, but you can't stop it. Deep down, all you want to do is cry out to God, the universe, or somebody, and say, "Why?! Why do I have to deal with this? Why doesn't somebody fix this, change it, or take it away?!"

Fair questions. Perhaps this really hard thing you are facing—this problem, this loss, this situation—is actually a test. It could be the biggest test of your life. But it's not like school. This is not about what you know. It's about who you are. It is a test of your character.

Maybe this painful circumstance is meant to weed out the idols in your life—those things you have trusted instead of God. Your looks, your intellect, your abilities, your personality, your family, your friends, your money, your connections—none of these things can solve this problem. God knows you have tried to make something happen, to fix it or stop it, but you can't. It's beyond your power.

You may have prayed a hundred times, "Take these circumstances away from me!" And certainly, God could. But God may choose not to do that. Maybe you are right where you need to be for some inside work to take place. Although God doesn't inflict painful situations on people, God doesn't waste them. If we allow it and choose not to turn away, God uses the really hard things that come our way to winnow out the dead branches in our lives, so we can grow strong and bear greater fruit. Like Abram, the disappointments and setbacks can serve to deepen our faith. Ironically, it's trusting through the wrong turns, the stumbling blocks, and the suffering they induce that enables us to persevere through the messy middle and see the comeback God has in store.

Amy, whose story started this chapter, had many opportunities to let God's work grow in her by love. She took a pass on every one of them until one night when someone got her attention. She was desperate for more drugs and was trying hard to get them when she heard a small whisper from God, "I love you and I have wonderful things planned for you. Get up and get moving." Two days later she ended up in rehab again.

"I think that is when the switch flipped," Amy said, referring to God's whisper. "Things were just different from that point forward. That last stint in rehab, I decided I was going to get on my knees every single night to thank God for my life and to show me another way."

Not long after, she was invited by friends to our church. She was stunned when she discovered that "there is a forgiving and loving God who will spread his mercy over me if only I am willing to surrender." Amy was baptized for the first time at age thirty-seven and joined the church. "Hands down, the best thing that has ever happened to me," she says. "Changed my life. Changed my heart."

But she is quick to add, "I'm still a work in progress, learning every day. I'm not where I want to be, but I'm definitely not where I was. Most days I want to scream from the rooftops how the grace of God has changed me. All the sins I have committed have been wiped clean. Words can't even describe this feeling. To know that he can forgive me made it much easier to forgive myself. Of course, I'm not proud of these things I have done, but because of the love and grace of Christ, I know that I have a lasting hope."

As you have gathered by now, letting go in trust, letting be in hope, and letting grow by love does not happen in a New York minute. You can't microwave this kind of transformation. It takes place in the long simmer of a slow cooker. Contrary to our fast-paced, high-tech world, true comebacks happen through the slow, seemingly inefficient practice of embracing patient trust.

Transforming Practice: Embrace Patient Trust

Patience is a lost art in the western world. We live in an on-demand culture. Fast food, same-day delivery, and instant access are bedrocks of twenty-first-century life. Waiting for anything—a rideshare to arrive, a text to send, or a website to load—is a sign that something has gone wrong, something that needs to be fixed, quickly. In a results-driven, time-starved world, practicing patient trust may be the one behavior we hate the most—and the most important. The world is full of things we can't make happen faster: friendships, winter, grief, a fine wine, love, and a little child telling a story. Embracing patient trust involves a willingness to let things develop in their own time instead of ours.

As much as we may want to hurry things along or fix a situation right now, there is often a different process at work, a slower one. In the middle of the last century, Pierre Teilhard de Chardin wrote a letter to his niece who was quite anxious about her future. It has become something of a prayer. Perhaps it would be a good prayer for us:

> Above all, trust in the slow work of God.
> We are quite naturally impatient in everything
> to reach the end without delay.
> We should like to skip the intermediate stages.
> We are impatient of being on the way to something
> unknown, something new.
> And yet it is the law of all progress
> that it is made by passing through
> some stages of instability—
> and that it may take a very long time.
>
> And so I think it is with you;
> your ideas mature gradually—let them grow,
> let them shape themselves, without undue haste.
> Don't try to force them on,
> as though you could be today what time
> (that is to say, grace and circumstances
> acting on your own good will)
> will make of you tomorrow.

Only God could say what this new spirit
gradually forming within you will be.
Give Our Lord the benefit of believing
that his hand is leading you,
and accept the anxiety of feeling yourself
in suspense and incomplete.[8]

As we make our way on the comeback trail, we are bound to hit snags and setbacks. Such disappointments are tests in disguise. They provide opportunities to deepen our faith for the long haul. When we get anxious and try to force our way forward (and we will), we'll have the inner resources to accept our incompleteness and to trust the process—even in the face of apparent failings.

By the way, twenty-five years after the promise, Abram and Sarah conceived and had a son. They named him Isaac, which means "he laughs." Soon after, God changed the name of this childless old man married to a woman past the age of child-bearing. God named him Abraham, which means "Father of many." Not only did Abraham become the father of the Jewish nation, but one of his descendants was Jesus Christ, who came to redeem and bless every family on earth.

For this highly anxious couple who ultimately trusted in the slow work of God, it was a comeback of miraculous proportions. As one biblical writer describes it, "And so from this one man, and he as good as dead, came descendants as numerous as the stars in the sky and as countless as the sand on the seashore."[9]

In the end, patient trust wins the day.

Conclusion

Coming Home

I could not quiet that pearly ache in my heart that I diagnosed as the cry of home.

—Pat Conroy

In the end, we return to the beginning. But it is a long journey back, with lots of ups and downs along the way. Life, if we are honest about it, is filled with falls. I had one just today. I didn't do something I said I was going to do, and now I have to make my way back with the people I disappointed. I wish this was an isolated incident. It is not. From what I can gather, I'm not alone. As the Bible describes it, falls of one kind or another began with the very first couple, Adam and Eve, and continue to this day. A quick glance at history confirms this unsettling pattern. Apparently, falls are woven into the fabric of human existence. Like little children learning to walk, we fall. Often. Ironically, the harder we try to avoid this fact, the more likely it is to occur. If given our preference, we would eliminate these pesky interruptions to our unrelenting climb to the top, but we cannot. They happen anyway, even against our best efforts. Author Richard Rohr gives a surprising explanation for this paradox:

> It is not that suffering or failure *might happen*, or that it will only happen to you if you are bad (which is what religious people often think), or that it will happen to the unfortunate, or to a few in other places, or that you can somehow by cleverness or righteousness avoid it. No, it will happen, and to you! Losing, failing, falling, sin, and the suffering that comes from those experiences—all of this is a necessary and even good part of the human journey.[1]

What? How can a fall be good? It depends on how we respond. If we will allow it, a fall can lead us on a journey home. Robert Frost wrote,

> Home is the place where, when you have to go there,
> They have to take you in.[2]

"So true," we say to ourselves with a smile, unless you happen to be the prodigal son. As he considered his return home, there were no guarantees. Let's take one last look at his journey.

It all starts with a fall. In blatant disregard for his father and his family, the younger son looked his father in the eye and demanded his share of the family's inheritance. To produce this sum, the father would have had to sell a third of his land, land he likely spent most of his life working to acquire. The idea was preposterous. But in a stunning turn, the father did so and gave the money to his younger son. The son quickly grabbed the cash and headed for a far country, where he promptly wasted every cent in self-indulgent living.

A turning point comes when a famine hits, and for the first time in his life, the younger son began to be in need. Too proud to admit defeat, he hired himself out to feed pigs. Standing in a field, hungry, dejected, and alone, he came to himself. In a sudden flash of insight, he remembered that his father's hired hands had plenty to eat. That's when he hatched a plan.

> I will set out and go back to my father and say to him: Father, I have sinned against heaven and against you. I am no longer worthy to be called your son; make me like one of your hired servants.
>
> Luke 15:18-19 (NIV)

Convinced he had solved his problem, he headed home. But the younger son was in a far country and the journey home was long. As he got closer, it surely crossed his mind that there were some holes in his plan. His father could refuse to see him. His father could be dead. His elder brother could banish him from the farm. Nothing was a given.

Regardless, the younger son soldiered on, trusting this was his best hope. In his mind, it checked all the boxes. In a culture steeped in honor and shame, he knew there was no way he could ever come back in the family. It would make his father the laughingstock of the community and add further insult to his family's name. The best he could do was sincerely apologize, humbly forfeit his right to be a son, and insist his father hire him. The plan really hinged on the father's response to his order: "make me like . . ." The verb there can also mean "to fashion out of." In that culture, hired servants could live as free men in the village and work for wages on a farm. Hired hand status would solve two problems for the younger son. He could live away from the seething anger of his elder brother, and most importantly, he could earn some money to pay back his father for the inheritance he had squandered. It was the perfect plan to make amends for his mistakes. He just couldn't have imagined the reception waiting for him.

While the son was still a long way off, the father saw him and ran to him, an outlandish action in that day. Children ran, perhaps young men, but mature men of stature? Not a chance. It was undignified. On that day, the father didn't care. When he reached his son, he threw his arms around him and kissed him.

On cue, the son started his well-rehearsed speech, "Father, I have sinned against heaven and against you. I am no longer worthy to be called your son." But the father cut him off. He turned to his servants, "Quick, bring the best robe," which would have been the father's robe. "Put a ring on his finger," a sign of authority, and put "sandals on his feet," because only slaves went barefoot.[3] In the whirlwind of activity, the son never had the chance to insist on a job. Just as well. The father had no intention of fashioning a hired servant out of this son he had longed to bring home. He called for the fattened calf to be killed and a feast to be held. He invited the whole village to honor his son. Yes, *honor* him. Why this neck-snapping turnaround? The father's reason ran deep. His son had been dead to him, but now he was alive. He was lost but now found. This comeback deserved a celebration![4]

Broke and broken, the younger son received immeasurably more from his father than he could have ever hoped—certainly far beyond what he had planned. When he returned home, it was not the same place he had left. It had changed because he had changed. Both the journey and his return transformed him.

The younger son needed the journey. He needed to taste the consequences of his own choices, to see how he had made a mess of things, to feel real need, and to finally come to himself. Even so, his comeback plan still included an attempt to save face, to be the one who rights his own wrongs and works off his own debts. His father's astonishing and lavish welcome changed all that.

Until the moment his father says, "Quick, bring the best robe," the son still plans to redeem himself as a hired hand. But before he knew it, the father had redeemed him as a son. To the son's utter surprise, his father's love could not be earned or deserved by good behavior, nor could it be lost by poor choices. It was a gift offered with no strings attached. For the first time, he tasted grace, and it changed him. For most of his life, the younger son had only wanted his father's things. After his return, he only wanted his father.

T. S. Eliot describes the journey this way:

> We shall not cease from exploration,
> and the end of all our exploring will be to arrive where we started
> and know the place for the first time.[5]

A change of heart changes everything. Remember our friend Shane, from the introduction? He carried so much brokenness in his life, he didn't know if he wanted to live or die. After an insane, nonstop drug fest one weekend, he thought he had shot up for the last time. But he hadn't. He says,

> When I woke up, that's when I knew there was a God. At first, I was kind of mad, and then it was confusion. How? Why? Obviously, there is a God, now it is up to me to figure why he kept me alive. What am I now going to do with this life?

Shane had been introduced to church and to Jesus a few times in his life, but it never took. Now, it wasn't a bunch of platitudes by church people. God was real, and for some reason, Shane was still alive. Did God have a purpose for him?

Shane soon jumped into a recovery program and over time got clean and sober. Out of the blue, sponsors and mentors saw something in him he could not see in himself. "We think you should be a pastor," they confided. Shane pushed back. He couldn't wrap his mind around it. After all that had happened to him, all he had done, he didn't feel worthy. But through prayer and the encouragement of wise guides in his life, he eventually decided they might be right.

After intensive training and mentoring, Shane now serves as the pastor of one of the largest Celebrate Recovery ministries in the Midwest. Each week, hundreds of people gather on Thursday nights to eat, worship, share testimonies, and meet in small groups. Many adults, youth, and families are receiving healing from hurts, habits, and hang-ups that used to enslave them. Shane says,

> It's been an amazing journey for me. A few short years ago, I would have never thought, "Hey, you are going to be a pastor of recovery." No, I'm not. I'm just a drug addict trying to figure out life. Now, I'm so blessed with this opportunity to say, "Hey, God can do this in your life, too. Life change is what it is about in anybody. Whether you are an addict or a co-dependent, you can find healing and freedom in Jesus.

This is the stuff of comebacks. It starts with a fall. You come to yourself. You find a wise guide. You plan and take action. And you trust the process. Each stage of the comeback journey involves key practices that help you move forward.

- Listen to your emotions.
- Choose solitude and stillness.
- Seek wise counsel.
- Plan and act.
- Embrace patient trust.

These five practices are designed for everyday people to make a turnaround from where they are to where they want to be. Anyone can do any one of them. However, true transformation comes when the practices are done collectively.

Now, let's be gut honest. We all know, not every comeback bid makes it over the top. Sometimes you still lose the game by a point. Sometimes you get down to the last two people and the job goes to someone else. Sometimes the marriage relationship simply can't be restored.

It would be tempting to see such experiences as more flops in a long line of falls. They are not. As you genuinely engage in the practices, they become seeds planted to bear fruit in a season yet to come. Granted, they don't feel that way in the moment. When a fall shatters our lives, it is very painful, but it's not the end of the story. God has a way of using the broken pieces to sow new hope on an unseen level. It may take years before it emerges, but it is growing even now.

A true comeback is not about outward results. It's about inner transformation. It's about who you have become on your journey home. On its deepest level, it's a redemption of the spirit and a restoration of the image of God in a human soul. It's expressed beautifully in Søren Kierkegaard's one-sentence prayer, "And now Lord, with your help I shall become myself."[6]

You will know you've made a comeback when you arrive at a familiar place and see it for the first time. Regardless of the score when the game ends, you know you did all you could, and you didn't let past mistakes or difficult circumstances define or defeat you. You rose above them. And knowing that gives you peace. True comebacks set you up for the next good thing to happen in your life.

In professional golf, there is a statistic called "bounce back." It measures how a player does on the hole immediately after he or she shoots over par. Will the player allow a poor score to get in his or her head and continue to play poorly or use that as motivation to get a better score on the next hole? What is really being measured is resilience.

In golf, as in life, the most important shot is the *next* one.

Now, let's head home.

Notes

Introduction

1. Scott Cacciola, "Cavaliers Defeat Warriors to Win Their First N.B.A. Title," *New York Times*, June 19, 2016, https://www.nytimes.com/2016/06/20/sports/basketball/golden-state-warriors-cleveland-cavaliers-nba-championship.html.

2. Joshua Berlinger and Jill Martin, "Cavaliers Win NBA Championship as LeBron James Has Game of His Life," CNN, June 20, 2016, https://www.cnn.com/2016/06/19/sport/nba-finals-game-7-cavaliers-warriors/index.html.

1. It Was Going So Well

1. Luke 15:13 (KJV).

2. See Luke 15:11-15 in the New Testament of the Bible.

3. Gregory Ellwood, "Review: 'Inside Out' Is Simply One of Pixar's Most Creative Films Ever," Uproxx, May 18, 2015, https://uproxx.com/hitfix/review-inside-out-is-simply-one-of-pixars-most-creative-films-ever/.

4. Peter Scazzero, *The Emotionally Healthy Church* (Grand Rapids: Zondervan, 2010), 83–84.

5. Max Lucado, speaking at the Promise Keepers Clergy Conference in Atlanta, GA, February 16, 1996.

6. Dan B. Allender and Tremper Longman III, *The Cry of the Soul: How Our Emotions Reveal Our Deepest Questions about God* (Dallas: Word, 1994), 24–25 (emphasis added).

7. George Hunter, *The Recovery of a Contagious Methodist Movement* (Nashville: Abingdon Press, 2012), 40.

8. C. S. Lewis, *Letters to Malcolm, Chiefly on Prayer* (New York: Harcourt, Brace, and World, 1964), 22.

9. Alice Fryling, *Seeking God Together: An Introduction to Group Spiritual Direction* (Downers Grove, IL: InterVarsity, 2009), 63–64.

10. Thomas Merton, quoted in "Seize the Day: Vocation, Calling, Work," *Reflections: A Magazine of Theological and Ethical Inquiry from Yale Divinity School*, Yale University, 2012, https://reflections.yale.edu/article/seize-day-vocation-calling-work/merton-prayer.

2. Coming to Yourself

1. Joshua Bains, "How to Cause a Paradigm Shift," September 23, 2016, https://medium.com/maqtoob-for-entrepreneurs/patricks-paradigm-shift-explained-with-golf-675b9b2cce02.

2. Joshua Bains, "How to Cause a Paradigm Shift."

3. Richard Rohr, *Falling Upward: A Spirituality for the Two Halves of Life* (San Francisco: Jossey-Bass, 2011), 12.

4. Stephen R. Covey, *The 8th Habit: From Effectiveness to Greatness* (New York: Free Press, 2004), 19.

5. Stephen R. Covey, *The 7 Habits of Highly Effective People* (New York: Simon and Schuster, 1989), 31.

6. Luke 15:17 (CEB).

7. Acts 9:1 (NRSV).

8. Acts 9:4-6 (NIV).

9. Acts 9:17 (NIV).

10. Eugene Peterson, *The Contemplative Pastor: Returning to the Art of Spiritual Direction* (Grand Rapids: Eerdmans, 1989), 18–19.

11. John Ortberg, *The Life You've Always Wanted: Spiritual Disciplines for Ordinary People* (Waterville, ME: Thorndike Press by arrangement with Zondervan Publishing House, 2005), 130.

12. Parker Palmer, *Let Your Life Speak: Listening for the Voice of Vocation* (San Francisco: Jossey-Bass, 2000), 10–11.

13. Stephen R. Covey, *The 7 Habits of Highly Effective People* (New York: Simon and Schuster, 1989), 89.

14. Melody Beattie, *The Language of Letting Go, Daily Meditations on Codependency* (New York: HarperCollins, 1990), 46.

15. Beattie, *The Language of Letting Go*, 46.

3. The Gift of Guidance

1. 2 Samuel 11:11 (NIV).

2. 2 Samuel 12:5 (NIV).

3. 2 Samuel 12:9-12.

4. Donald Miller, *Building a Story Brand: Clarify Your Message So Customers Will Listen* (New York: HarperCollins Leadership, 2017), 73–75.

5. Gil Gruber, "Discovering the 4 Panes of the Johari Window for 360 Degree Feedback," *Explorance*, August 26, 2013, https://explorance.com/blog/discovering-blind-spots-in-360-degree-feedback-with-the-johari-window/.

6. Romans 7:15 (NRSV).

7. Luke 15:17-19 (paraphrased).

8. John 16:13 (CEB).

9. Richard Foster, *Celebration of Discipline: The Path to Spiritual Growth* (San Francisco: Harper, 2000), xx.

10. Romans 3:23 (NIV).

4. Hope-Filled Action

1. "Haiti Earthquake Fast Facts," CNN, last updated January 14, 2020, https://www.cnn.com/2013/12/12/world/haiti-earthquake-fast-facts/index.html.

2. Richard Pallardy, "2010 Haiti Earthquake," last updated January 5, 2020, https://www.britannica.com/event/2010-Haiti-earthquake.

3. Michael Hyatt, Best Year Ever audio series, 2017.

4. Peter Scazzero, *The Emotionally Healthy Leader: How Transforming Your Inner Life Will Deeply Transform Your Church, Team, and The World* (Grand Rapids: Zondervan, 2015), 66.

5. Luke 15:17 (NRSV).

6. Henry Cloud, Facebook, January 1, 2020, https://www.facebook.com/DrHenryCloud/posts/we-change-our-behavior-when-the-pain-of-staying-the-same-becomes-greater-than-th/10154915434634571/.

7. Simon Sinek, *Start with Why: How Great Leaders Inspire Everyone to Take Action* (New York: Penguin, 2009), 39.

8. Sinek, *Start with Why*, 39.

9. Sinek, *Start with Why*, 40–41.

10. Gail Hyatt, https://michaelhyatt.com/photos/people-lose-their-way-when-they-lose-their-why-gail-hyatt/.

11. Maya Angelou, *I Know Why the Caged Bird Sings* (New York: Ballantine Books, 2009).

12. Nelson Searcy and Kerrick Thomas, *Launch: Starting a New Church from Scratch* (Grand Rapids: Baker, 2017), 56–58.

13. Greg McKeown, *Essentialism: The Disciplined Pursuit of Less* (New York: Crown Business, 2014), 195.

14. Karl Weick, "Small Wins: Redefining the Scale of Social Problems," *American Psychologist*, 39, no. 1 (January 1984): 40.

15. Weick, "Small Wins," 43.

16. Weick, "Small Wins," 43.

17. School of Hope (website), accessed February 2, 2020, https://schoolofhopehaiti.org/the-vision.

18. School of Hope (website), accessed February 2, 2020, https://schoolofhopehaiti.org/the-vision.

5. Trust the Process

1. Francis Dorff, *The Art of Passingover* (New York: Paulist, 1988), 39–40.

2. Gerhard Von Rad, *Genesis, Revised Edition: A Commentary* (Louisville: Westminster John Knox, 1973), 159.

3. David Westin, "Tiger Woods Wins 2019 Masters Tournament," April 14, 2019, http://www.augusta.com/masters/story/news/2019-04-14/tiger-woods-wins-2019-masters-tournament.

4. Wikipedia, s.v. "List of career achievements by Tiger Woods," last accessed February 2, 2020, https://en.wikipedia.org/wiki/List_of_career_achievements_by_Tiger_Woods.

5. Brennan Manning, *Ruthless Trust: The Ragamuffin's Path to God* (New York: HarperOne, 2000), 5.

6. Dan Wetzel, "How Tom Brady Engineered the Greatest Super Bowl Comeback Ever," Yahoo Sports, February 6, 2017, https://sports.yahoo.com/news/how-tom-brady-engineered-the-greatest-super-bowl-comeback-ever-072553731.html?guccounter=1&guce_referrer=aHR0cHM6Ly93d3cuZ29vZ2xlLmNvbS8&guce_referrer_sig=AQAAAMTxxPXfgcesKnLQijqcofDbxdkvaHPofuohADnEk_p-fNSMJS9Qj5l7CvsykiEu6yLybkSLQwHNicA1glw86COM8_vtZeEUKIR5QcRtUUdEEraTauFYAlX5G4BK6jYtQVmM5WijDftbEuevnQQiCNiA0wPaFRqIZgN6RVse-7m1.

7. Kevin DeVries, "Trust the Process," *Grace Explorations*, February 2017 e-newsletter, https://graceexplorations.com/media/.

8. Pierre Teilhard de Chardin, "Patient Trust," *Hearts on Fire: Praying with Jesuits*, ed. Michael Harter (Chicago: Loyola Press, 2005), 102.

9. Hebrews 11:12 (NIV).

Conclusion

1. Richard Rohr, *Falling Upward: A Spirituality for the Two Halves of Life* (San Francisco: Jossey-Bass, 2011), xx.

2. Robert Frost, "The Death of the Hired Man," *North of Boston* (New York: Henry Holt, 1914), 20.

3. Luke 15:21-22 (NIV), selections from the verses.

4. Luke 15:23-24.

5. T. S. Eliot, *Four Quartets* (Orlando: Harcourt, 1943, renewed 1971), 240.

6. John Ortberg, *The Life You've Always Wanted: Spiritual Disciplines for Ordinary People* (Grand Rapids: Zondervan, 2002), 14.